PRAISE FOR *Worldly Girls*

"Tamara Jong has written a deliciously subversive book about ideologies which allow us to survive while also imprisoning us. A brave set of storied memories about growing up with a Nova Scotian mother who raised her as a Jehovah's Witness and a Chinese immigrant father who resisted, this book is about growing up in the in-between space: what we anchor to when there are few absolutes and how we move beyond the ties which bind to find our own path forward. This book is an ode to the examined life and a roadmap to ultimately defining who we are on our terms, informed but not bound by our ancestry. A delightful addition to the memoir canon."
—Annahid Dashtgard, author of *Bones of Belonging* and *Breaking the Ocean*

"In *Worldly Girls*, Tamara Jong writes with clear-eyed honesty and emotional intelligence about the intertwined ties of family and religion. More than a memoir, this book is a tribute to women everywhere who struggle with love, depression, our relationships with our mothers and with motherhood itself. In other words, *Worldly Girls* is for all of us."
—Jen Sookfong Lee, author of *Superfan*

“Tamara Jong’s memoir *Wordly Girls* is a glistening mosaic of memory. Arranged in sharp and vibrant fragments, Jong explores the jagged divisions that break and shape us, and the love that can unite us beyond faith, time, and life. This story is sharp and soft; a razor’s edge to your tender heart. An unforgettable read.”

—Hollay Ghadery, award-winning author of *Fuse*

My family at my parents' wedding reception in Chomedey, Laval, Quebec, April 24th, 1971. Back row, left to right: my Ma (Alexandra), my father (Thomas), my little brother Tommy. Front row, left to right: me, my oldest sister Angie.

WORLDLY TAMARA

GIRLS

A MEMOIR IN ESSAYS

JONG

ESSAIS SERIES NO. 18

BOOK*HUG PRESS
TORONTO 2025

FIRST EDITION

Library and Archives Canada Cataloguing in Publication
Title: Worldly girls / Tamara Jong.
Names: Jong, Tamara, author.
Series: Essais (Toronto, Ont.)
Description: Series statement: Essais series
Identifiers: Canadiana (print) 20250205696 | Canadiana (ebook) 2025020570X
ISBN 9781771669504 (softcover) | ISBN 9781771669535 (EPUB)
Subjects: LCSH: Jong, Tamara. | LCSH: Jong, Tamara—Childhood and youth.
LCSH: Jong, Tamara—
Family. | LCSH: Ex-church members—Jehovah's Witnesses—Biography.
LCGFT: Autobiographies.
Classification: LCC BX8527.J66 A3 2025 | DDC 289.9/2092—dc23

The production of this book was made possible through the generous assistance of the Canada Council for the Arts and the Ontario Arts Council. Book*hug Press also acknowledges the support of the Government of Canada through the Canada Book Fund and the Government of Ontario through the Ontario Book Publishing Tax Credit and the Ontario Book Fund.

Book*hug Press acknowledges that the land on which we operate is the traditional territory of many nations, including the Mississaugas of the Credit, the Anishnabeg, the Chippewa, the Haudenosaunee, and the Wendat peoples. We recognize the enduring presence of many diverse First Nations, Inuit, and Métis peoples, and are grateful for the opportunity to meet and work on this territory.

To Ed and S, you changed my life.

To my parents, the original storytellers.

Worldly

1. An individual who does not follow Jehovah and his laws, who pursues materialism, higher education, and fleshly desires, and who chooses the "philosophy and empty deception according to human tradition" (Col. 2:8). A non-worshipper, unbeliever, outsider, someone who is "bad association" that can lead a Christian astray from Jehovah. "An enemy of God" (James 4:4).

2. Experienced or sophisticated.

CONTENTS

Some of the names of individuals in this book have been changed or aren't provided/ given at all. These tellings are my own and remembered to the best of my ability. At times, I may have recalled what others have said through my own lens.

TRIPTYCH: WHAT WE GET TO KEEP

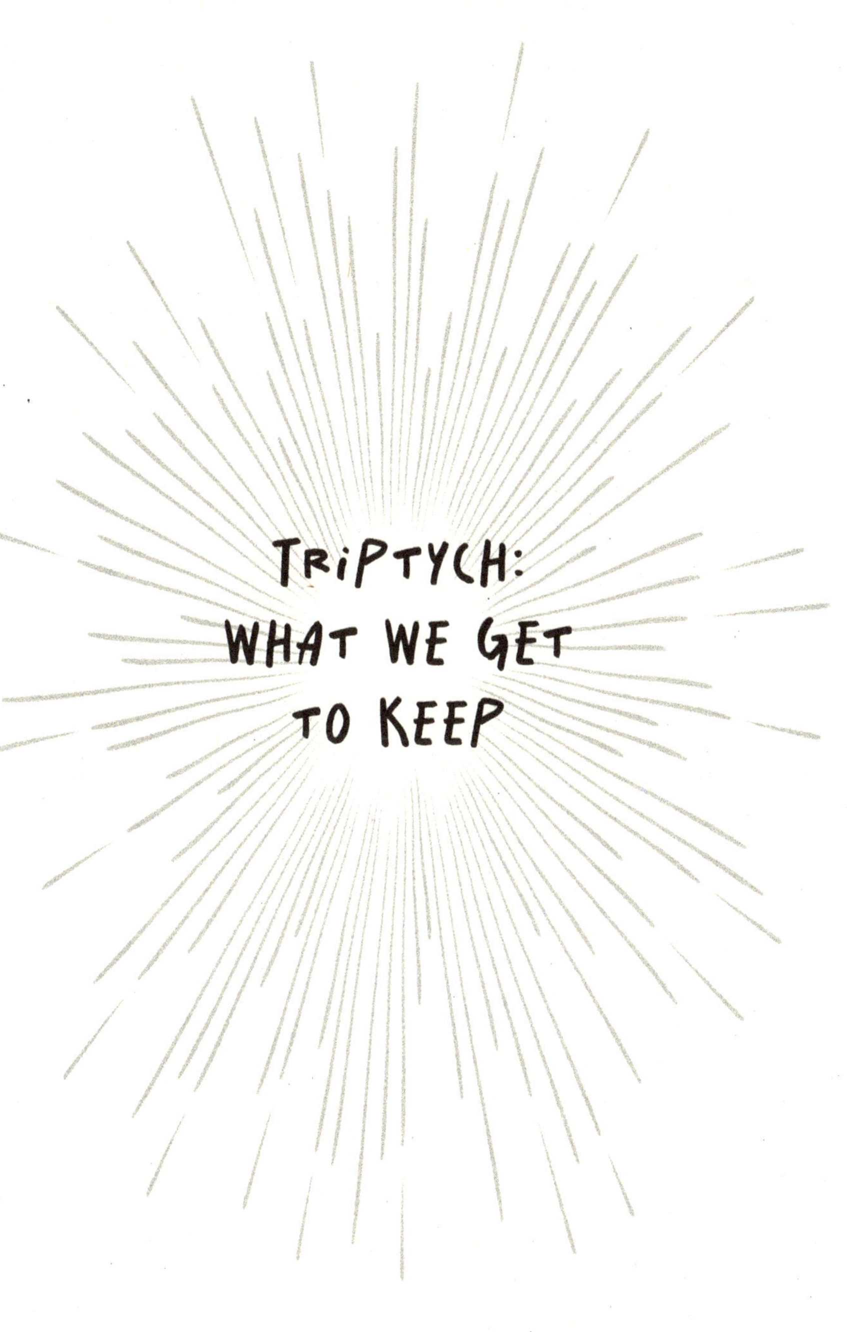

1.

When I was in kindergarten I wrote a story about my family. There wasn't much of a plot. I depicted them as tiny, smiling, round-headed people obsessed with cleaning. I drew detailed pictures of our plumbing, the car, the oven—even the coin-operated laundromat in our building, the dryer visibly tumbling clothes round and round.

In the story, my sister sorts the chaos of shoes near the front door of our tiny apartment. I'm at the kitchen counter putting away dishes, while Ma, with a drawn-on smile, is vacuuming the rug, little speckles of loose dirt making their way up into her treasured humming beige Electrolux. (I would eventually inherit Ma's drawn-on smile, among other things.) My brother only appeared on the cover, too tiny to contribute.

Ma and us girls were in dresses because, for those growing up Jehovah's Witness, the teachings advised that "women should adorn themselves in appropriate dress, with modesty and soundness of mind…but in the way that is proper for women professing devotion to God, namely, through good works" (1 Tim. 2:9, 10).

. . .

My father always told us about everything that needed to be cleaned and what needed to be avoided altogether: money, shoes, motel rooms, beds, bathrooms, door handles, and my uncles, Ma's brothers.

"Don't hug or kiss them," he would say.

We once saw our Uncle Alec blow his nose into a paper bag and throw the bag under our coffee table. Alec would play silly card games with me when he visited, which was never really for long. He was probably passing the time before going back to New Waterford. Ma was always wanting to help her brothers—or anyone really. That was always her way, which may have attracted her to the ministry in the first place.

Of all our assigned chores, I liked vacuuming the most. Something about it calmed me, the way it drowned out the world and sucked away all the filth. The sound of the dirt going up through the hose was so satisfying, even if the carpets and floors would only be clean for a few hours. My father bought the vacuum from a door-to-door salesman, and it cost a lot of money on some kind of payment plan.

When Ma was younger she used to wipe her bum with old newspapers in the family's outhouse, and her brothers and sisters had to share shoes so they could take turns going to school. Ma was so proud of that vacuum. She must have thought she'd finally made it.

. . .

I was twenty when Ma drowned in Cancun, and her prized possession, her vacuum, came to me. Of course, I also got other things when she died: jewelry, childhood photographs, a sectional couch, some household items, and her unpublished poetry.

My sister never asked for any of Ma's things. When she later asked to borrow Ma's vacuum cleaner for a while, I didn't hesitate. When I wanted it back, she told me it didn't work anymore and was beyond repair.

It would be years before I got another vacuum. When I did, it wasn't new, just someone else's second-best, which I rightly deserved.

II.

"Do not think I came to bring peace to the earth; I came to bring, not peace to the earth; but a sword. For I came to cause division, with a man against his father, a daughter against her mother, and a daughter-in-law against her mother-in-law. Indeed, a man's enemies will be persons of his own household. Whoever has greater affection for father or mother than for me is not worthy of me; and whoever has great affection for son or daughter than for me is not worthy of me" (Matt. 10:34–37).

. . .

When I was little, Ma was ministering to a sister from Kingdom Hall whose husband had been disfellowshipped and expelled from our congregation. When my sister, brother, and I played hide-and-seek, the husband scooped me up in his arms to hide me in a good place. Since I didn't want to be "a sharer in his wicked works" (2 John 1:11), I didn't say a peep to him. I was good at following the rules.

When Ma got disfellowshipped for smoking, Ray, a long-time elder and friend of the family, called me before the official announcement. I cried while holding hands with my friend Natasha at the closing prayer. I knew that if Armageddon came tomorrow, Ma would be washed away with the rest of the wicked world because she no longer had the mark that Ezekiel 9:4 speaks of.

"Jehovah said to him: 'Go through the city, through Jerusalem, and put a mark on the foreheads of the men who are sighing and groaning over all the detestable things that are being done in the city.'"

Ma had survived a terrible childhood but couldn't part with her Du Mauriers.

When I turned eighteen, my sister and I moved out. Since I recently became a full-time minister, I had to protect my spiritual life and heart from Ma. Jehovah had always been my constant, and I owed Him this. Prayers and hopes for Ma's repentance and a return to Jehovah and His loving congregation never came.

The last time I saw Ma alive, we didn't speak. We were both in Montréal, in the underground tunnel leading to the Métro Henri-Bourassa. Ma was going to her job at a nursing home, and I was heading back to Laval after my cleaning job. It was rush hour, just another mundane morning, and people were shuffling past one another.

I hadn't seen Ma for months and now here she was, standing right in front of me, waving. I wasn't at all prepared to shun her and was mindful of Apostle Matthew's words—"the spirit of course, is eager, but the flesh is weak." My mind often works in the scriptures. I felt closest to Matthew, a despised tax collector who sacrificed everything to follow his Lord. When Matthew scribed

Jesus's life, there was a contradiction; Jesus was to fulfill prophecy by dying for humanity, yet he asked for the cup to be taken away, crying out to God in his final moments. Maybe I wanted to tell my Witness friends that I kept going, that Ma repented because I maintained my integrity.

I would write and rewrite this scene in the subway many times in the years that followed, but I rarely told anyone that I waved back.

III.

I have been recently hospitalized for depression, just like Ma was, except I'm thirty-two and she was thirty-eight. I never thought I would end up where she had been—me, the ideal workaholic, a Kingdom Hall–going Jehovah's Witness.

But here I am, back in my friend Robin's house, on the hard blue cement floor of the bathroom, with the door shut, plucking out my sparse arm hairs one by one with my good set of tweezers, something that always seems to relax me.

Time moves slower. My mornings and nights are unscheduled, seemingly unending. I barely pray or study, and there are nightmares.

I go to three weekly Bible meetings at the Kingdom Hall because Robin refuses to leave me at home alone. I can't blame her after I tried to hang myself in her basement, which is what got me hospitalized in the first place. I wonder if things would have been different if I hadn't said anything.

I'm not much different than teenage me—I need to always have that best friend. There were times when I didn't have one, and I was so lonely. I wonder how much of a burden I am to Robin, who is now livid on the other side of the bathroom door.

She's mad because I took apart her vacuum, piece by piece. I worked my way through the filter and motor, and gave them a good scrub, but now it won't work. She is yelling at me, and I barely understand what she's saying, yelling back at her to leave me alone. I don't normally yell. My nerves aren't great; I am visibly shaking.

I remember once Ma chased me and Tommy with a butter knife down our apartment hall to the bathroom. We both ran, screaming the whole time, and scrambled to lock the door.

I rarely cry these days, but today the tears I've held in all year don't want to stop.

Robin is afraid I'll hurt myself. Of course, she is right to worry and now refuses to leave. I know I can't win this argument with her, so I push past her out of the bathroom and curl myself into a loose ball on my bed in a dark corner of this dingy little basement. The light from the bathroom lets me see the outline of her body, and I feel her sit at the foot of my bed. But we're still so far apart.

There's a brief moment when I think, *God, when was the last time we even laughed together?* Gone are the nights we stayed up talking until dawn. We are strangers now. Robin stopped telling me important things—how her marriage was falling apart, and she had started to fall apart too. At thirty-two, I didn't know that I'd be leaving the Jehovah's Witnesses in five years. I didn't know that my faith in God would wane and fade.

I didn't think I'd be losing Robin.

I was trying to repair the vacuum, but I knew nothing about vacuums. I didn't know that I never would be able to fix what I had taken apart.

LESSONS

One, two, buckle my shoe.

In kindergarten, when Miss Steiner took out the wooden shoe with its demonic yellow laces, I'd hide with the dust bunnies under my desk.

I didn't know how to tie my shoes. I tried to learn, but it just wouldn't stick in my brain. Miss Steiner noted this lack on my report card. Turns out teachers cared if you couldn't tie your shoelaces, but nitrate-laced hot dogs for lunch were hunky-dory.

(Miss Steiner told Ma that I had memorized "We Are Jehovah's Witnesses," and then had the whole class singing it, so I guess I could do some stuff all right.)

At the Kingdom Hall we learned about Armageddon, and Satan, and what happens to those who do not follow God. Lying was forbidden because Jehovah sees all, and I could pray to Him when tested. To make us good Christians, Ma often read to us from the book *Listening to the Great Teacher*, but it didn't always work. For example, when Miss Steiner said it was okay for me to eat pumpkin seeds at Halloween, I believed her. Ma punished me for that with her hand on my backside. It was one of the many times I failed her and God's rules.

Unfortunately for me, Velcro sneakers didn't become a thing until the eighties, so I struggled to tie my shoes way after kindergarten. I was at least eight when my father finally taught me while we waited for our clothes to be washed in our apartment building's laundry room. (I cling to those early memories of him, before he left us.) Even with his help, it took me forever to figure out where the laces went and how to make a knot that stayed tied up. I had trouble listening to directions. I needed to see it. *Show me*, I'd say.

Some believer, huh?

I learned early to disguise who I was, whether it was hiding under the mask of being a Jehovah's Witness, concealing not getting math concepts and being bad at shoelace tying, or pretending to be fine no matter what—especially when it came to my parents' troubled marriage. (The fights. Oh, the fights.)

We never talked about my mother's problematic drinking, only endured it silently.

Children always seem to be good at hiding what is not ready to be seen.

. . .

Three, four, knock at the door.

I'm twenty years old when Crystal tells me about a stranger who came up to her when she was steps away from the Kingdom Hall.

"Why do Jehovah's Witness girls wear hooker boots?" he asks.

I met Crystal at a party when I was sixteen. We hit it off right away. She was everything I wanted to be as a Witness. She was funny, decent, kind, and a great friend, but we aren't in the same hall. Even if we were apart, we knew every Saturday morning we had our routine; we'd be knocking on doors with our Bible-based magazines—*The Watchtower* and *Awake!*—preaching the Kingdom message.

I always started with my memorized conversation starter, the one I had spent time preparing at home, practicing in the doorway that separated the kitchen from the hallway. If I could throw in a scripture, I did. I really liked Revelation 21:4, New World Translation: "He will wipe out every tear from their eyes, and death will be no more, neither will mourning nor outcry nor pain be anymore. The former things have passed away."

A typical introduction at the door would go something like this: *How are you today? We're just taking a moment and sharing with our neighbours a message about God's Kingdom.*

(Do not mention Armageddon yet. DO NOT mention Armageddon yet.)

Gauging their interest, I would offer a magazine or a book, and make a note to return in my "return visit" book. I would then call on them and call on them until they either accepted a Bible study or told me not to come by anymore.

I grew up on a regular, steady diet of "everyone wicked dies at Armageddon, except those doing God's will." First, Jehovah told Jesus that, and then Jesus told the elders and ministerial servants (male shepherds chosen by the holy spirit and the Governing Body of Jehovah's Witnesses). The shepherds were always male, blessed, and living in a volunteer commune supported by voluntary donations from the flock. (Long live the patriarchy.)

When I started drifting away, it was 2005. I was depressed again, and my belief system was falling apart. Therapy was beginning to heal me in ways that had me thinking about possibilities other than religion and God. Living apart from the congregation and the weekly meetings started to whittle away their hold on me.

Yet despite all these years of separation, I find myself on many Saturday mornings feeling that I need to be somewhere else. On a nice sunny day, I think, *What a nice day for service.*

Also, whenever I pass a pair of Witnesses standing by their cart of publications—and for some reason I see them a lot—I think, *That could be me. That* was *me.*

...

Back in my Jehovah's Witness days, I wanted to be one of God's best students. I needed a dad when mine was absent, even if he was an invisible one.

If I had been born around the 1930s during the bombastic preaching days, I would have put on one of those placards that read "Religion Is a Snare and a Racket!" I would have worn my sensible shoes and lugged around that twenty-one-pound phonograph so you, too, could hear the good news of God. I've sometimes considered that if a leader told me to drink the Kool-Aid, I would have done that too, if that's what I thought God wanted.

Now, away from the flock, the pang of God guilt hovers around the back of my brain, and I wonder if I've made a mistake leaving the Jehovah's Witnesses. It was a safe place for a mixed-race person like me. I wasn't an outsider. All the pictures in the Jehovah's Witness literature—besides the destruction at Armageddon—had everyone from different cultures in harmony. Racism couldn't possibly exist in God's organization. No one treated my Chinese dad as different. He would've told us, wouldn't he?

(But I do recall that the question "Where are you from?" still cropped up occasionally.)

My friend Rachelle, who has also left, says when chimps get excluded from the community their chances of survival statistically diminish. I've yet to join another church, and even though signs from prophets are of the past, I long to see one.

Here I am, searching for my community again. Religion was my life, and now there's this void. I don't know where I belong these days. I've always followed someone else's rules.

Maybe if I discover who I am, I won't like what I see.

...

Five, six, pick up sticks.

When I invite my best friend Robin to my upcoming wedding, she refuses to come. Robin and I first met when I moved from Laval to Ontario, and we became fast friends. And now, after years of friendship, it seems like I am throwing it all away. Robin is clear; she's not coming because I left the Jehovah's Witnesses and my leaving has interfered with our friendship. She says I have chosen a way of life without God, and that has saddened and disappointed her.

Sticks and stones may break my bones, but words will never hurt me.

Meh. I would rather have the stoning already.

...

I don't know why I'm standing in the cold at Robin's front door at eight o'clock at night, two days before I get married, in black boots that Ed, my fiancé, gave me. I've been crying all week when really I should be happy. Ed has no idea how busted up I feel inside. I break out into tears any time I hear Rihanna's "Stay," listening to her describe a love that is painfully coming to an end.

There's a Reddit-post theory on the song that suggests it's about a girl who lost her faith in God.

I've had two hours of therapy this week. My therapist has said to put these hurt feelings away for now, but I just can't. I've never read a story like Robin's and mine, though I know it must exist. I expected that a boy would break my heart, and he did, but not like this—a happy moment overshadowed by the grief of losing my friend.

I'm the type of person who has said it's so sophomoric to have a best friend. I know I've said so many stupid things. I want to tell her that I need her, miss her, and can't remember anything in the last fifteen years without her in it. Doesn't that count for something?

I also know this drill. I've done what Robin is doing to me now—to my sister, to my mother, and to one of my other best friends. I am considered bad association now. "Do not be misled. Bad associations spoil useful habits" (1 Cor. 15:33). I know it's not personal; it's God's rules or the highway. I am asking Robin to love me more than she loves God, and ultimatums rarely work.

. . .

We're standing in Robin's kitchen.

"I've come to say goodbye," I say.

I can tell she didn't understand, so I continue.

"I don't even know if I believe in a God anymore."

. . .

Wait, I'm wrong—we're in her doorway, and I'm leaving. See how my memory betrays me?

She is telling me she won't give up on me. "I have enough faith for the both of us," she says as she cries.

I can't speak. I can't say what I actually think out loud to her, so I hug her. Twice.

I want to yell it out for anyone to hear. There isn't enough faith in the universe to bring me back to her, to the congregation, to Jehovah. I'm sorry. There will be no going back.

When I tell my therapist that I impulsively drove to Robin's to see her one last time, she seems surprised. She tells me that of course I *had* to go. She describes how Robin has been like a mother to me, and when she says it, every part of me realizes that this is true. I am coming face to face with losing not only my god, my faith, my religion, but my mother again. Always my mother.

I finally understand how my mother unravelled. I'm sorry, Ma, I just didn't know.

. . .

Seven, eight, lay them straight.

I have a hard time buying boots. I tried to get boots at this one store and tried on twenty fucking pairs but couldn't zip half of them up. My calves are too big, and so are my sister's.

I blame my father. My father is a stocky sort of guy, and his calves are big.

I blame my mother for the fundamental religious bullshit. My dad never converted.

. . .

Nine, ten, a big fat hen.

Chicken shit. Coffee grounds. Tea bags. Apple peels. A steady diet of compostable goodies for the gods, and if the gods today are, say, a flock of hens and one ball-busting rooster, then it's all good.

I am staying at a Jungian therapist's B&B. I've been helping out with the chickens and getting the eggs in the early morning, but I'm afraid of the rooster. Whenever I come close to the pen, he stalks me and keeps making this weird noise that unnerves me. I am the outsider, and he wants to make sure I know who is in charge, and it sure as hell ain't me.

The B&B is home to a dog named Shadow. Jung says that the shadow is our repressed unconscious, and that getting to know our shadow is the way to individuality. The dog Shadow comes around my cabin and takes strolls with me. When we get sprayed by a skunk, the smell is everywhere, and I am so embarrassed. It smells for days. Shadow has never been sprayed before, the Jungian therapist tells me.

One day Shadow chases a deer into the forest, and I call for him to stop, to please come back. I would follow, but I don't know the way. I'm afraid to get lost.

I'm reading too much into this—it's just a dog being a dog. He's not leading me away from God or safety. But I don't want to admit that lately I've been feeling unsteady in my faith, that I no longer can approach God and have it be a comfort.

. . .

When I don't have enough money for therapy, my therapist tells me to come in anyway. It is hard for me to accept this gift. In between sessions, I feel unanchored, my thought patterns spinning out of control. I listen to loud, angry music and write autobiographical fiction that has "beautiful language, but nothing seems to happen." (Comments I will get years later in my first writing workshop.)

While watching *Napoleon Dynamite,* I slice my hairless forearm with a silver box cutter, but only make some very superficial scratches. When my therapist asks me if she can see the marks, showing her makes me feel safe. She assures me that going back on antidepressants will only turn the volume down on my anxiety and depression, reminding me that I'm not a failure of a human being.

She counts my sorries during our hour together and wants to know why I keep apologizing for being on this earth.

(The number is fourteen.)

Is it cliché to say that I can never pay her back? To say she saved my life in a way Jesus never could?

. . .

Ma let us know her family was Catholic and poor, that there were seventeen of them, and that she and her siblings had an abusive childhood. Her dad used to hit them all pretty regularly and loved his racehorses more than kin. When my uncles Alec and Peter were grown-ups, they went back to see their dad and beat him so bad he couldn't walk.

Ma ran away from the farm at twelve.

Auntie Marg told me that all the kids in their family were writers. (On my daddy's side, there's a doctor and Taoist monk, but no scribblers.) How much of Ma's side or my father's side is me, and how much of my former Jehovah's Witness faith is still me, it's hard to say.

I grew up outside the city, but my husband calls me a city girl. I loved going to farms and petting zoos when I was little, but that's not me anymore. I'm not used to seeing animals, except for hermetically sealed ones in pretty packages in the grocery store.

My father used to make us give him the fat off our plates—he loved to eat it off the bone. I remember seeing him sucking on chicken feet, not wasting the juice. When I went to dim sum with him, a lady took the chicken feet off her cart and placed them on our table, saying I'd like them if I tried them. I sucked the juice off of the wrinkled feet just like my father did. I didn't know I was supposed to eat the skin until I hit the bone.

I miss my father's cooking and who he was when I was a child—not who he became when my parents divorced.

. . .

It's time to get the eggs again. I look at my watch alarm and, for a second, think about hiding out in bed, but instead I decide to get my butt up and at 'em. The chickens peck at my boots when I get past the squeaky gate. The rooster eyes me up, inching closer. I try to pretend I'm not scared, but I can't stop sweating.

When I was barely eighteen, I was out preaching door to door when this rooster attacked me and my preacher buddy Di. He got huge, spreading out his wings, and we could see his claws, toes, spurs—everything. He took a run at Di, and she swung her bookbag full of *The Watchtower* and *Awake!* magazines at him like a shield. I was of no use, running away to the opposite side of the street, just watching, not knowing what to do, hiding in plain sight (something I had learned well from those shoelace school days).

When finally a random car drove up the road and separated us from this fighting rooster, we didn't continue preaching but preferred the safety of Di's car. I was so young and inexperienced then. I didn't know that by running away, I only did what I needed to do to save myself.

I tell myself it's going to be okay, that this rooster in the here and now is not the one from my past. I'll be slow, deliberate, and let the rooster see me, but if he thinks I am leaving the coop without those eggs, he's wrong.

I didn't come all this way just to leave with nothing.

THE BURNING

In 1973, I headed off to kindergarten for the first time. Martinvale Elementary School was a twenty-minute bus ride away and one of the few English schools in Chomedey, Québec. My parents spoke English at home. My white ma hailed from New Waterford, Nova Scotia, and my dad from a small village in Taishan, Canton, China. I had shoulder-length brown hair and brown eyes—definitely my dad's kid.

It frightened me to be apart from my older sister, Angie, her school another distant bus ride away. My baby brother, Tommy—the spoiled favourite—got to be at home with Ma. When I finally got home from school, I just wanted to be with her, too, but she would set me down for a nap—she needed those regular breaks to catch her breath.

At the Kingdom Hall of Jehovah's Witnesses, we were the "Jong Kids," mostly said with an eye roll and an exasperated sigh. We were energetic little bundles, running wild in and around all the brothers and sisters, under and through their unsuspecting legs. At home, we loved to drive our toy tractors through the living room and kitchen, round and round wherever there was space in our tiny one-and-one-half apartment, probably driving the neighbours below us mad.

When Ma took Tommy to the doctor for a checkup he said, "Mrs. Jong, most kids get tired after running in circles. Your son runs circles around those circles." I always kept up with Tommy, but Ma never took me to a doctor. I followed my little brother everywhere, even though I was the older one. I was a lot quieter, so it was hard to figure out if there was something wrong with me.

Maybe Ma saw something in me that resembled her, a trigger of a sort that took her back to childhood.

...

We didn't have many toys growing up, but the ones we did have were scattered around our shared bedroom. One day, all the toys in the room disappeared, except my teddy bear, Panda. We knew better than to ask why. We had been careless and messy, and this was a warning.

Panda was my beloved companion, with his eyeless, noseless face, and a gigantic safety pin to keep his pink underwear on his body. His white fur was no longer white, the threads in his neck were unravelled, his black hair hard and stiff, his stuffing sparse. The day the toys disappeared, Ma held him up in front of me and told me that she was going to toss him in the garbage. My grief was instant. I imagined him burnt up in the fires at the bottom of the trash chute.

Ma made no promises of a new teddy to replace him, no bribes if I was good and took my nap. Maybe she thought that toys were a luxury she never had, her childhood being one where food was not on the table and love was not an option, but being beaten was. Perhaps she thought I was a spoiled, weak thing, and that this was one of many hard lessons I needed to learn. Or maybe she resented Panda because I had him to hold on to when Ma could not give me the love I needed.

Ma's say was final, and I silently cried when I went to go take my nap. Had I whined out loud, it would have only invited smacks. (When her hand got too sore, she would move on to wooden spoons, the belt, or the orange Hot Wheels track instead.)

When I got up from my nap, Ma handed Panda back to me. He was not ashes in the incinerator in the basement of our fifteen-storey apartment. Instead, she had sewn Panda two new blue button eyes, and a nose from thick bright pink knitting yarn. She had repaired his Frankenstein monster neck.

Ma never spoke of any favourite doll or teddy. When she talked about her childhood, there were only stories of lack. Nobody was coming to save Ma and her siblings; they had to save themselves. We never met her father, Ma made damn sure of that. When Ma's mother came to visit, no one called her *Grandma*. Ma said it would be weird. When Ma returned to New Waterford as an adult, she stood outside the house she had grown up in and could not will herself to go inside.

I realize now Ma had tried to break the cycle in her own way, by pretending to hurt me through Panda. Perhaps Ma saw herself in me, even though I was only five years old. Perhaps she knew I was the sensitive one who clung to her too much, that I would never be as tough as her.

Perhaps she knew that the shadows of her childhood were intertwined with my own, and that she may as well toss everything I ever had down to the bottom of that chute, where the fire turned everything to ash.

DEAR CHARLY

July 12th, 1981
Dear Charly,

It was good to see you in the halls at Chomedey High today. It's been a while, and I remember how difficult it was to have a conversation at the Kingdom Hall because everyone was always trying to talk to you.

When you first moved to the congregation, it was exciting to have someone there we hadn't grown up with. It's like you get comfortable with whoever is around because you have no one else. I did have a best friend back in kindergarten—Gisela—but she moved away to Pierrefonds. We met up a few times after that. We saw the movie *Grease* at the Cinéma Kirkland. But then I broke her dad's bike and never saw her again.

Anyway. Ma has never been overly keen on me having too many friends that aren't in the truth. Ma would be okay if you came over because of the Jehovah's Witness connection. She likes you, and she doesn't always like my friends. She's always sure to tell me what's wrong with them.

I feel like our family came to your place once, didn't we? Usually, we have the JW brothers and sisters over to our apartment, where my dad cooks for everybody, but my parents aren't real sociable these days. I'd still like you to come hang out, just us.

I want to show you the room Angie and I share, with the wall-to-wall posters we're pretty proud of. Rob Lowe, Rex Smith, John Schneider, Bruce Lee, Gary Carter, Doug Risebrough, and Youppi! Do you have any posters in your room? Tommy shares a room with my parents, but it's mostly his.

Our building has like seventeen floors. We're across the water from the creepy-looking convent complex, Soeurs de Miséricorde. You may be shocked, but we used to yell things like "God is dead!" when we saw the nuns strolling along the walkway. That's no way for a Jehovah's Witness to act. Please don't tell Ma. She may drag out the belt again, even if I am fourteen. I've smartened up a little since those early days.

Where I live, at Bellerive, the three apartment buildings together resemble something sorta like the Trinity to me. They're right off the Rivière des Prairies. I like staring at the water, even if it looks murky. There's something about it that's relaxing. I lose track of time just standing at the edge of the building promenade, looking at the water. Do you have someplace you go to relax?

I was kinda surprised when you told me about the boys we know smoking weed. Aren't they baptized? My sister doesn't believe it, says it's impossible. I used to like some of them, too, but the boys see me just as the little kid sister. Did they smoke up at the Police concert? I gave the boys two bucks to get me a program. Maybe they think they can do whatever they want before they get baptized.

Angie got baptized at ten because Ma pushed her to and the elders felt she was ready. I mean, Jehovah's always watching. If I do something wrong, I'd be afraid someone from the congregation might see me, plus Satan is always tempting us, too, if you think about it.

Angie started to date somebody in the hall. He says I give him dirty looks but I don't. That's just my look. Oh, and I have a secret, too, since you spilled that one about the boys smoking weed. I dated one of those brothers in the group too—secretly. I hadn't been baptized yet, so I guess I thought it was allowed.

The brother said he loved me, and I was naive enough to believe him. We passed notes, talked behind the Kingdom Hall in the dark, hid it from his parents, and kissed a bunch. I read his letters over and over again and hid them in a binoculars box so no one could find them. All of a sudden, he wouldn't take my calls or see me, and I didn't even know what I did. Then I saw him holding hands with a chick from our school. I was so mad, but what was I going to say? I mean, we hid it from everyone.

I had been so careful about who I liked. I wondered how feeling broken in so many places was possible.

I hope you don't mind me writing to you, Charly. I know you're older than me and way cooler. And you have a boyfriend, so you know about all this stuff.

Are you going to go to college? Angie is in her last year of high school and wants to go to Vanier. She says she'll take something easy like psychology. Sounds like a bore to me. I like drawing cartoons, so maybe I'll apply to some graphic design program. We keep hearing how using our youth in the ministry is better than pursuing higher education. I guess I gotta think about it. Big choices.

Is drama with Mrs. Moss a breeze? You seem like you'd be good at it. I couldn't act in any play, especially in front of our high school. I guess you can't care what they think.

. . .

We don't live far from the Parc Belmont, the amusement park, so if you come over we can walk over the Pont Lachapelle instead of taking the bus. We do it all the time so we don't have to pay two fares. I can show you the hole in the fence where kids sneak into the park for free. We won't do that, though. I have some babysitting money, so we can go on a few rides.

Did you know they have a recording booth at the park? For two bucks, Tommy and I sang Blondie's "Call Me." We laughed so hard when we listened to it on the record player. All you can hear is Tommy's high-pitched voice, which drowns mine out. The song is on the *American Gigolo* soundtrack, dix-huit ans et plus. Can you imagine?

Once, this older guy followed me across the Pont Lachapelle and tried to put his arm around me. I jumped about ten feet. He said, "Je veux manger ton cul." Being polite, I said, "Pardon?" And the perv repeated it! I told him he was disgusting and ran away, but my heart was beating so hard. I don't even know if I told Ma about it.

Ma told me a man followed her on her way home one night across the bridge, but then there was a thunderstorm, and he disappeared. I remember Ma came home in soaked white overalls.

We all keep going over the bridge anyway. If you don't have the extra dough for the bus, you gotta do what you gotta do.

. . .

Two weird smells I like are the musty garage in our apartment building and the smell of the river water under the bridge—even if it looks grey and polluted, and you can see dead fish from time to time. Tommy told me he climbed down there once just for kicks. His friends are nothing but trouble. Worldly boys, but hey, I wasn't studying the Bible with Steve and Cherie yet, so I hung out with Tommy's friends a little.

Once, Tommy's best friend Dean dared me to steal a toy snake, which was easy. He also offered me a cigarette, and it tasted gross. Once, in grade 3, when Mrs. Vandenburg forced me to do math in front of the whole class, I cried and Dean tried to whisper the answer to me. Mrs. Vandenburg was super tall with brown curly hair and orthopaedic shoes. We called her "Vampire Bat" behind her back.

I stopped hanging out with Tommy and the boys when they started breaking lights in the garage of one of the nearby apartment buildings. I mean if you ask me it's not exactly clever to vandalize the buildings you live in. When we got chased by the super and I got caught, Tommy was the only one to come back and get me. The super asked Tommy if he'd like it if he came to his house and broke his TV. Tommy told him he wouldn't mind, but his ten brothers wouldn't like it, so the super let us go.

Who'd think fourteen-year-old me would be following a little twelve-year-old kid around? As Tommy would say, *I'm a fool.* I know you think he's a cute little kid, but don't let his smile fool you—he gets into all kinds of trouble. He even laughs when Ma spanks him with the wooden spoon.

I'm glad I have Steve and Cherie. Things can be weird at home with my parents, and Steve and Cherie treat me like their kid, act like parents are supposed to. They want to know how I'm doing in school and don't nag me. I love Cherie's kids. I want to be a mom one day and have five kids at least.

Sometimes, Dad sleeps on the couch. He works most nights and weekends, but when he is home, Ma likes him to cook.

Sometimes, my parents yell, and it's hard to sleep. Our bedroom door is just like thin cardboard. One night my dad punched it instead of Ma.

We've been in this building for at least ten years. My parents had had enough of the cockroaches in the last apartment they rented in downtown Montréal and how they had to sleep on the floor in the kitchen. Dad said they were poor. We moved to Bellerive when we were real small—they got a one-and-a-half, and we all slept in the same room. It was wall-to-wall beds, and all of our toys would get stuffed underneath them. I don't remember there being any drawers for our clothes. It was pretty sparse in there. Just plain white walls and no carpet, with high windows, dusty shelves, and a big closet.

Our apartment was so small that when Angie got chicken pox, Ma told Tommy and me not to play with her, but we did anyway. We ran naked around the place, getting water everywhere from the baking-soda bath Ma drew to stop the itching. Ma was so mad that she had to chase us around. Then she slipped and fell in it. We laughed so hard. We really got the licks that day.

Our new apartment is better and bigger. I've got space for my *Charlie Brown* and *Archie* comic collection. We've got a radio in our room to listen to American Top 40. I was convinced rock bands lived in our radio when I was little. I tried to look inside, but there was nothing to see.

I have this gut feeling we won't see each other for a long time after you leave school and this place for good. You'll be on to other things, and I will too. Maybe one day I'll see your name at a feminist art conference in Toronto—you'll be on a panel, and I'll run into you in the line to see the exhibitions. You'll remember me for reasons I still don't understand, and you'll show me

Haley Craw's artwork *Apostasy in Practice*. We'll instantly know the Jehovah's Witness books in the installation—the iconic blue *Truth* book, *Family Life*, and the ol' golden *My Book of Bible Stories*. She's us, or was us at one time, and we're her.

Maybe you'll never see this letter, because I haven't written it until now.

LISTENING TO THE GREAT TEACHER MIGHT GET YOUR ASS KICKED

My first fight with Ma was over a boy—a baby boy. It was 1969, I was two, and my bratty little brother, Tommy, was on his way. I already didn't like him much.

There were signs that the little prince was coming. A multicoloured terry cloth Humpty Dumpty doll was sitting in a new white crib, out of reach of the soon-to-be-forgotten baby—me. Our tiny apartment on Rue Dutrisac in Saint-Laurent, Québec, would grow smaller still.

Everything was changing. Ma had taken up with the Jehovah's Witnesses, and now this little kid was arriving to mess up my world, to put me smack in the middle of the dreaded sibling pecking order. It had been me and my older sister, Angie, and that's the way I liked it.

After Tommy was born, I didn't talk to Ma for two weeks, my anger slowly fermenting. At least this was what my dad told me. I was so mad that I refused to speak to her, even though I was so attached to her—too attached, it would seem. I was a jealous little thing.

I never really fought with my dad. I was too afraid of him, at least before my parents divorced. We were all terrified of Dad because it was belts on our asses if we acted up. Dad always bragged that he was some karate expert, training that he began as a boy in Taishan, Guangdong, China.

(He told me he was young when he left, that the village's name escaped him. I wondered how you could forget where you grew up, how you could erase your early beginnings.)

My siblings and I would joyfully hang off our dad's muscular arms, our skinny little fingers holding on tight. It was rare to see him not well put together, every black oil-slicked hair strategically in place. One time this neighbourhood bully dared us to "go on, get your dad" and Dad flexed his muscles happily. He could never back down from putting on a show. Dad regularly wrestled my brother while laughing hysterically, baring his pink gums and the gaps his false teeth left behind. Ma also sported a pair of false teeth, hers grinning nightly from their perch in a glass on the bathroom shelf.

Ma fought for every scrap of her life, even to the end of her forty-three years. She ran away from New Waterford to Toronto at twelve, the city where she would later meet my dad. My Auntie Marg told me Ma spent time in juvenile detention centres and foster homes. She learned to tuck in sheets at boarding school and named my sister Angela Frances after two nuns who had been kind—a rarity back then, I realize.

Ma was a real-life Doris Day movie-star type with blond hair and hazel eyes. Dad said she jumped over a restaurant counter once when someone called him a slur, fixing to beat the girl for being racist.

When I was growing up, I respected and feared my sister Angie. She is two years older, and we shared the same double bed until we moved out of Ma's. When I was a teenager she burned my forehead with the pink and white Crazy Baby curling iron, the damn steam holes leaving marks on my skin. She always seemed frustrated, the stand-in parent when Ma couldn't deal with us. We were a lot, I know, when she had to be the stand-in parent.

It's always been hard for me to yell because of my parents, seeing Ma drunk, and watching the arguments leading up to the divorce. When I got married to Ed, I didn't realize that fighting with your spouse could be normal. I'd freeze, waiting quietly until I was ready to move on but inside wanting so badly to throw a plate.

When Ed and I fought, I wondered if our relationship was over, where I would live, whose couch I could sleep on. Ed finally told me that fighting does not mean he hates me. That people work it out. My parents couldn't, but we're not them.

My therapist once asked me to scream into a pillow. I tried, but nothing came out.

...

I wish I were tough like Ma was, but anger always shrinks me down, leaving me tiny. I'm often full of fear and freeze. I also didn't inherit her poetic stylings, but would write as a white protagonist instead of a Chinese and white girl. Growing up, I read anything I could get my hands on—cereal boxes, *The Montreal Star*, *The Gazette*, *Anne of Green Gables*, *Superman* and *Archie* comics.

Like Ma, I became a Jehovah's Witness, indoctrinated from my toddler days. Going to meetings three times a week, going door to door, going to ministry school and studying the Bible made me a faithful devotee. These leanings should have brought Ma and me closer together but didn't.

When I was thirteen, Ma hit me in the head because I backtalked her. Angie had been on the phone and Ma demanded she end the call, that she tell whoever was on the other end that there was a problem in the house and she needed to say goodbye. Angie told her friend that our mother was the problem in the house. I laughed and Ma hit me with the telephone. Angie jumped her and it cost her a black eye.

Angie ran away for part of the evening, and when she crept back in hours later she didn't mention what had happened. She told her friends that she fell down the apartment stairs.

There were many times I would pick a fight with Ma, too many to mention. Once I told her she was the worst mother in the world, so clichéd and unoriginal of me, a writer's sin. As soon as I spoke the words, they were like acid on my tongue, something I could never take back no matter how many times I said I was sorry.

As a teenager, I wanted out of my so-called family. I felt like Ma had driven my dad away with her drinking and need for a divorce, and I wanted her to pay. I wanted to be a daddy's girl but was unaware that my dad didn't want me to be a daddy's girl.

...

In one of my favourite books, *Listening to the Great Teacher*, former tax collector Matthew quotes Jesus. "However, I say to you: Do not resist him that is wicked; but whoever slaps you on your right cheek, turn the other also to him" (Matt. 5:39). Jehovah's Witness kids aspired to be like Jesus, studying in the temple, always righteous, obeying our parents and God. But Jesus could call legions of angels to defend him instantly, so he had that in his back pocket.

I've noticed that specific types of anger mean repercussions, at least for women. God fought with Adam and Eve, but it was Eve who got the brunt of it with childbirth pains and periods. If we were created in God's image, why did Eve have to suffer more? If that's not passive-aggressive anger, then I don't know what is.

Anger was allowed when Jesus chased the money-changers out of the temple because they made it a house of commerce. When I got older it felt right for me to angrily tell Ma that her smoking was bad and her resistance to quitting showed her lack of love for God and us. She annoyed me in the ways families tend to do—her dirty ashtrays around the house, borrowing my clothes without asking, and the never-ending tea-bag graveyard that she left just sitting on spoons on various surfaces. We'd fight about her new boyfriends after my parents' divorce—especially Bob, who was the one we liked best, but were mad at because he was married.

It seemed Ma never had trouble finding replacements for our dad.

. . .

My last fight with my brother Tommy before I left home for good was initially over the television remote. He ended up calling Angie a "fat cow" and then I was between them, yelling "Fuck!" which was very un-Jehovah's Witness-like. I slapped Tommy in the face hard, and he punched me in the throat. I hit the floor and heard Angie say, "Look, now you've killed her."

My voice disappeared for days. Nothing would come out when I tried to talk. Perhaps my voice holds that memory still.

. . .

When I was eighteen, Ma was finally disfellowshipped and cast out of the Jehovah's Witnesses for smoking. If I were to continue living with her, a person who, according to the Apostle Peter in 2 Peter 2:22, had "returned to her vomit," then I wouldn't be doing what God told me to do. I pushed Angie to move out with me, and we went to live with a married couple who were told by the congregation's brothers and sisters that Jehovah would bless them for taking us in.

Ma wasn't there on our move-out day. After we left, she tried calling occasionally, but I knew we were supposed to limit our contact. My faith would be proved by putting God first, and I deserved His love. I felt God was proud of the choices I made for Him.

When Ma died, she didn't have a funeral service in the Kingdom Hall, but my Uncle Danny, an elder, gave the memorial service. According to the Bible, some people do not get into paradise when they die; those who have taken their own lives, those who have sinned against the holy spirit, and the disfellowshipped. Some sister from the Kingdom Hall told me that my mother would not return in the resurrection.

"I know," I told her without judgment.

My anger and grief over Ma took more than twenty years to appear. I always thought God knew what was best for me and that I didn't need her. I became furious with God, but it didn't matter. God was offering me conditional love, and it wasn't enough. My parents had taught us to survive without them, and I could survive without God.

Once I had stopped going to my Jehovah's Witness meetings, I wondered about my purpose. I got jobs in customer service, administration, marketing, and waitressing. Between therapy and meeting my husband, Ed, my former religion was pushed out of the way. Any Jehovah's Witness would tell me I couldn't find meaning because I'd left God out of my life and no longer associated with His congregation.

While I respect other people's views, religion just doesn't feel like something I can commit to anymore. I feel like serving someone else means losing too much. Writing is the only thing I can give all of myself to without holding back. I hope Ma would be proud of me for that.

. . .

I once found a dime on the carpet at work, and I put it on my desk and forgot about it. Later, I came across an article that said finding a dime means a dead loved one is trying to contact you and that the date on the coin has significance. I couldn't wait to see what message I would uncover, but by the time I returned to the desk to look for it, the dime was already gone.

I left things bad with Ma, and there is no fixing that. But I think I am starting to forgive myself.

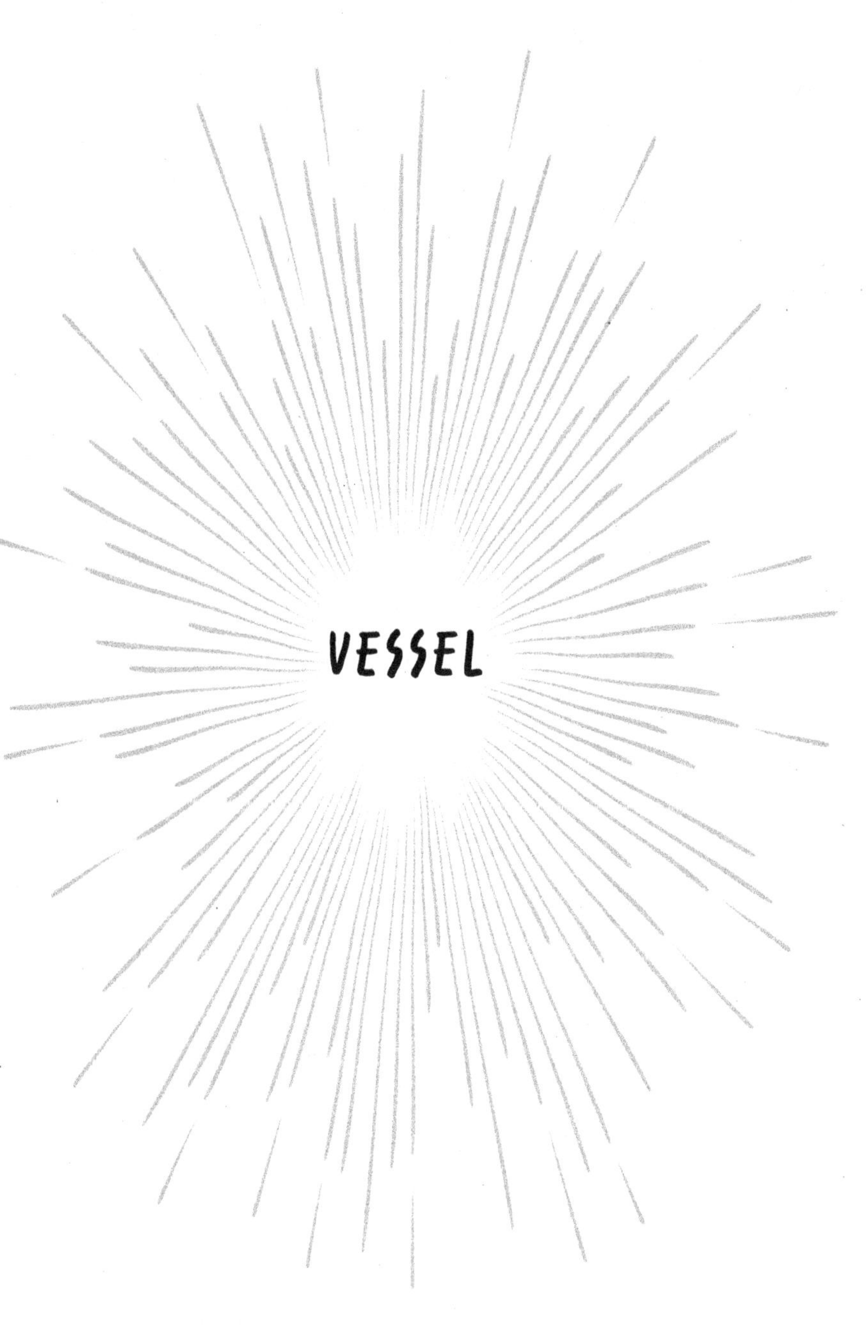

VESSEL

Much like my delayed shoe tying, I couldn't tell the time for the first five years I was in school. I struggled with math, and the numbers on the clock only confused me. I had this Snoopy watch I loved, mainly because the minute hand was a tennis ball. I got by okay by bluffing my way through with my Consumers Distributing digital watch. I even fooled my parents somehow, but maybe because of their own drama, they didn't notice I couldn't tell time.

When I was twenty, I got the watch Ma had on her before she died. I studied it for a long time before I stuffed it in my drawer. It's a gold-coloured Timex, the lustre faded, adding to its charm. It has a small oval face, stick bar markers instead of numbers, and a stretch band that used to catch the little blond hairs on her wrist.

Some parts of me act as a reminder of Ma. My voice, my laugh, my expressions. My sister, Angie, and my father tell me this. When I look in the mirror, I struggle to see what they see.

Ma's boyfriend, Owen, paid for their trip to Cancun, taking my little brother, Tommy, along. Ma was going to pay him back. On the plane, Ma told Tommy that she had insurance in case anything happened to her. It was a sunny, hot day when Ma gave Owen her watch and keys to take care of while she and my brother went for a swim. I wish Owen had gone instead.

When I get the watch, it is given to me in a plastic sandwich bag.

. . .

I've only kept a few of Ma's belongings since she died. I have handfuls of her old family photos, the ones that Aunties Marg and Diane claim she took from them. I feel guilty about wanting to keep them but not guilty enough to return them. It's easy to keep what belongs to another when you have shouldered mountains of regret.

Ma was a poet, and Auntie Marg said one of Ma's poems was about drowning. My brother told me he found another one of Ma's poems that only had four lines. I'm not a poet, so I don't know if it was any good.

I once contacted Concordia to see if there were records of Ma's poetry from back when she was a student, but since she was no Mordecai Richler, no one replied.

. . .

My sister and I didn't have much of a relationship with Ma later in her life. We let God's laws separate us.

My sister said maybe Ma's watch came back with her luggage from Cancun, which ended up in her Saint-Laurent apartment. Ma had asked me to clean her place while she was on vacation. I said no, but planned to anyway because she was my mother.

That doesn't matter now.

. . .

When it was time to clear out Ma's apartment after she died, my father came along. Dad was quiet a lot of the time we were there with him. He ended up keeping one of her favourite John Abbot College sweatshirts. He started crying at her kitchen table and said that she was the only woman for him. I had never seen him this way, and it shook me. Ma divorced my father when I was fifteen and effectively divorced us kids too. In many ways, God had replaced my father, standing in for him when it felt like he had abandoned us. My love for God would alter and betray me, but at twenty, I knew everything and, of course, nothing.

Maybe it took us hours or days to go through everything in Ma's apartment. I can't remember. It was exhausting to sort through her memories. We didn't ask my brother to help us—he was only eighteen and still in shock. He was the one who had tried to save her from drowning. He would later wonder aloud why it was her and not him. In some ways, he's drowning still.

I still don't know how I came to receive the watch. Did my brother give it to me when he got off the plane from Cancun at Mirabel? When I asked him about it, he said he was sorry, it was all a blur. I remember watching my mother's coffin roll across the runway. My brother says Owen packed all of Ma's stuff. Maybe Owen gave me the watch after he bawled in my arms.

Although I scour my memory, it remains an unreliable narrator.

Owen had asked Ma's brothers and sisters at the funeral to pay him back for Ma's part of the trip. Later, we received a lawyer's letter from him that told us Ma's couch was his and he wanted it back. My Uncle Peter wanted to kill Owen and stuff him into a car trunk.

...

Ma drowned on Tuesday, April 14th, 1987, after lunch, seven days before her forty-fourth birthday. Somebody rescued her, but the paramedics had not been able to stabilize her, so she died on the way to the hospital. The death certificate would say this. My friend translated the words for me since they were in Spanish. She said that it was written like a story.

When I take Ma's watch out of the plastic sandwich bag for the first time, the hands show it's just before six in the evening. I pull the crown, but the battery is dead. I sniff the watch and then I sniff it again. It doesn't smell like Ma. Ma's purse used to smell like cigarettes and Wrigley's Spearmint gum. I can still remember the scent.

FiCTiON
BABY

At eighteen, you wanted to get hitched to Peter. It's the Jehovah's Witness way, and you wanted out of your family ever since you'd been born into it. But then your feet turned into blocks of ice because you were straight up terrified to be anyone's anything.

You should've had five kids by now, a good-sized Christian family. Though your therapist doesn't like the word *should.* When she talks you listen because her words cost "you're not covered by company benefits" money. Maybe she can figure out what's so wrong with you.

With straight red hair, freckles, and the broadest shoulders you'd ever seen, Peter was your rebound guy. Dancing to every slow song at that party, you forgot Noah had broken your sixteen-year-old heart. Noah was supposed to be some kind of diary-story crush, but instead you made a no-kissing rule that you stuck to way before Julia Roberts's character in *Pretty Woman* said she doesn't kiss on the lips and made it a thing.

You always fell for the whitest guy in the room. You didn't want anything to do with your dark-haired, brown-eyed, short, mixed-race self. Your heart was full of all those Jane Austen happily-ever-afters. When Noah avoided you at the Kingdom

Hall, when he wouldn't take your calls and stopped giving you love notes, you just kept reading his letters, the ones hidden in the binoculars box, and wondered what you did wrong.

When Noah moved away, you hoped to heal. You knew you'd never be seen as a grown-up in this God-forsaken town of Chomedey, so you moved to Port Perry after all your blah-blahing about never leaving Québec. You missed your siblings and were barely speaking French, an anglophone with a high school education and a dead mom.

Noah friended you on Facebook twenty-five years later, after your friend married his little brother. You had to be a bridesmaid and pretend you were okay, realizing you could never get away from the first person who hurt you.

Noah told you via Facebook Messenger that he barely knew his reasons for breaking your heart, that he struggled with depression now and then, and there had been times when he wanted to talk to you about what had happened. Still, he was just a teenager when he hurt you, and what little truth he was saying may have been a lie to spare your feelings.

It made you happy to tell him you couldn't do dinner; he was one of your first loves, and you wouldn't want your hubby hanging out with an ex-girlfriend, and you're not even the jealous type.

. . .

Rebound Peter made you want to have his red-headed kidlets. He filled the hole in your seventeen-year-old heart with enough love notes, gifts, and photographs to stuff a Hefty bag. You ended it with him by writing some fool letter saying you wanted to preach full-time and weren't really in love, that you think you'd know if you were in love by now and pretty soon, he'd realize that he wasn't either.

You remember yourself in the last apartment you would ever share with Ma, in your bedroom, definitely not falling in love with Peter, stretching the limits of the beige telephone's cord across your bed, pulling the cord to your desk, and onto the apartment balcony, all because you could never sit still. You would talk to him for hours about everything and nothing.

Now when the radio plays "Two Less Lonely People in the World" by Air Supply, you can still see the two of you sitting and singing on a park bench in N.D.G., wishing that son he's so proud of was yours too.

you'd know if you were in love by now and [illegible] pretty sure [illegible] either.

[illegible] yourself in the living room [illegible] share with Mark, your bed [illegible] with a ter, examining the walls of the beige [illegible] across your bed, pulling the cord to your desk, and onto the apartment balcony, all because [illegible] still. You could talk to him for hours about everything and nothing.

Back when [illegible] plans "[illegible] Love [illegible]" [illegible]
[illegible]

LITTLE
SAVIOUR

My baby was going to be my Jesus Christ. My baby was going to save me.

Oh, I know it sounds blasphemous—no one has to tell me this. The residual religious part of me lingers and rears up every now and then. The scriptures still come to me, but my internal judge and jury? Well, they're less active these days. Besides, I married the first guy I slept with and am no longer living in sin.

I wanted to wait to have a baby until Ed and I got hitched, God approved. There were also other factors: we needed more money, there was always gonna be one more writing course to take, or I needed to change jobs. We had my seven-year-old stepdaughter, Avery, in our lives, and even if parts of me were kind of broken, I had loved her since she was a baby.

Ed told me it was time to stop with the excuses. There would never be perfect conditions for a baby. I knew my clock wasn't just ticking; it was two minutes to midnight. We had stopped using birth control since the wedding, but maybe forty-six-year-old eggs just wanted to retire. Maybe they were comfortable with their fancy cups of tea and a good book.

...

When I was ten years old my Barbie dolls had an exciting life inspired by a steady diet of the soap opera *Another World*. Barbie and Ken were in a blended family. Ken had custody of a son from a previous marriage, Barbie, a teenage daughter, and the pair had a new baby together. Ken was the breadwinner, and Barbie stayed home and took care of the kids. Ken often fought off the advances of a much older, beautiful cougar Barbie next door. The fam vacationed at the beach on the tattered end of the green carpet in our two-and-a-half apartment in Laval, Québec.

When I was fifteen, my father left and started a new family. By then I was too old for make-believe.

In my 1984 high school yearbook, I wrote that my ambition was to be a wife and the mother of five kids. I got baptized that year, took a vow to Jehovah, and became a Jehovah's Witness. I was a good Christian girl, and we didn't casually date—only when we were ready for marriage. Being a good Christian girl also meant no drunkenness, blood transfusions, voting, joining the army, or taking drugs. If you doubted if you should, you just didn't.

My parents' unstable marriage had come undone, so it made me wary of relationships as I got older. I often wondered if I had any idea what a good relationship was, but I still hoped that when I figured it out, the babies would come. That I'd get my happily ever after.

...

At thirty-eight, I drifted away from religion after a lengthy depression, antidepressants, and therapy, but I was still going to JW meetings on and off. The elders from my hall had visited me on a shepherding call I can now barely remember. I had been seeing my Jungian therapist twice a week, and my thinking had changed. I had reached many lows, but therapy was working.

My job in sales wasn't what I wanted to do with my life, and I left it for a new one in marketing. It was 2006, a new start. My co-workers were pleasant and welcomed me in. They became good friends of mine and helped me navigate the world. I had lost much of my former community, so I decided to pursue my dream of playing in a ladies' hockey league. I wasn't good, but it didn't matter. I was ready to try anything, even if I was terrible at it.

That year, I met Ed through his best friend John, who worked with me at the new gig. My car had a broken thermostat and John said his best friend Ed was a mechanic and that he could fix it for me. I didn't know that he was setting us up.

John invited me to play golf with Ed and him and then cancelled on us at the last minute. Ed was a shy introvert and definitely just my type: a blond-haired, green-eyed hockey fan who wore a Vancouver Canucks retro ball cap. I thought he was cute, and we had fun. My original plan to return to the Jehovah's Witnesses started to fade into the rear-view.

Ed told me that he had broken up with his girlfriend, Lori, and that she was pregnant. He was nervous but wanted to be a father. He would be there for them even if he wasn't in a relationship with her anymore. I was drawn to Ed because of this. I hadn't planned to love him and his new little girl, but it happened, and eight years later, I married him in a civil ceremony. (I couldn't do a church even then.)

At first, the idea of me as a stepmom seemed fine. I had always loved kids. Avery already had a mom, and we shared custody. But my little ward triggered me, and the memories of my alcoholic, religious Ma and my emotionally distant, disciplinarian father affected my parenting skills.

If I did have a baby, would it be a semi-functional mess like me?

My thoughts about becoming a mother unearthed so much grief. My new therapist convinced me in session after session that it wouldn't be so awful to have me as a mom, that the mistakes my parents made didn't have to be my mistakes, and that I had a healthy, stable relationship with Ed.

Eventually, she sold motherhood to me, and my reservations slipped away. My heart swelled.

My world now consisted of cycle-tracking, pregnancy tests from the dollar store, and an ovulation app reminder. The possibility seemed real. I didn't want to admit that I had hoped for this ever since I was a little girl, that I had been hanging on to this wish for so long and that part of me was afraid of disappointment.

...

I ask the baby if I should quit my job so we can have a better environment for an anxiety-free pregnancy.

This is my window, says the baby.

We're running out of time, says the baby.

I tell the baby I don't know what a real mother looks or smells like. I'm only a stepmom, a glorified babysitter. Part of me thinks that I will most likely fail in this quest. My faith used to be my strong suit, but it isn't anymore.

I tell the baby that when I say *I love you* to my stepdaughter, it tastes foreign, like when I had been driving past Milton and a tractor-trailer had flipped across the lanes on the 401 and caught on fire, and all I could taste was plastic on my lips.

I tell the baby that I can't remember when my mother told me she loved me, that the doctor told me I might have twins even without fertility drugs, that they would split me open and give me a C-section because of my age.

I tell the baby that it didn't sound negotiable nor pleasant.

I tell the baby I am worried.

The baby says, *My name will be Hans-Peter.* I start to laugh and say that won't work. What if you're a girl?

He says he just wants me to hold him.

We can do this, he tells me. *It will just take some work and planning.*

He says he's been waiting for me to decide and stop with the excuses. If only I'd believe.

Yes, I tell the baby, *if only.*

This baby is smarter than I am.

. . .

Seven months later there have been no positive tests, no pregnancy, not even an *Am I? Could it be?* moment. I think I must not have believed enough. Surely this is my punishment for having left Jehovah.

. . .

I am surrounded by babies and pregnant women everywhere. Lori tells me she is obsessed with getting pregnant again, that she and her husband have been trying for years. I distract myself by reading *Frankenstein* and watching shows like *Stalker*, *The Honorable Woman*, and *The Walking Dead.*

I thought that once I had decided, it would be easy. I'm forty-six. I have been a fool, I guess.

At my annual physical, my doctor quizzes me about baby making.

"Are you and your husband still thinking about having a baby? Where are you on that?"

She quickly glances at me and then continues to type on the keyboard furiously. Her brown purse is slung across her chest like she is a gunfighter.

"We've been tracking my ovulation cycle."

"Menopause happens at forty-eight and up. Have you thought about going to a fertility clinic? I can write a referral."

"I'll talk to Ed."

"Well, you need to do it soon. You don't have to come in again. Just call, and we'll let them know. Do you have any clinics in mind?"

Ed had told me that if I couldn't get pregnant right away, he didn't want fertility treatments.

"Do you want a house or a baby?" he said.

We've wanted a house for so long—a place to put down some roots. My parents never owned a house. My sister owned a house. My brother owned a house, then separated from his wife and gave her the house, then moved to Nunavut, returned, slept on my couch in my apartment, and then moved into someone else's house.

"No. I don't have a clinic in mind."

"You will gain weight if you have a baby."

"I know."

Her eyes blink rapidly behind her black-rimmed glasses.

"There is always adoption."

"Yes."

"But then there can be issues with that as well."

"I'll talk to Ed."

Ed says it won't hurt us to see what the clinic offers. A referral is made, and the clinic will call me with details. It feels like so much waiting.

. . .

I checked my voice mail every day for two weeks. Finally, the fertility clinic left me a message.

I returned the call to the clinic while I was at work, and the VP kept walking in to talk to me as the clinic receptionist kept going on about directions like it was the first time I'd ever left my home. I was barely listening to her as I wrote illegibly on useless, too small yellow Post-its.

Ed came with me to the initial appointment. Part of me was worried he was just trying to please me. No one knew we were hoping to have a baby, except Lori—not even my in-laws or any of my friends had an idea that we went to a clinic. I didn't want them to judge me for wanting a baby at my age.

When we walked through the clinic doors, I told Ed I felt like a loser. He said many couples go to fertility clinics. It's common. We saw only one other couple filling out forms and heard the many televisions, all on the same channel, echoing between the waiting rooms. Paper towels were strewn all over the floor in the bathroom, and the walls were an ugly orange. There was a picture of a poorly drawn toilet on the back of the bathroom door with the words *Flush the Toilet* printed underneath.

What am I doing here?

We had many forms to fill out, but my list of questions was longer than Ed's. He showed me a question about a descended testicle, and we started laughing. Then we debated about how often we have sex, and I wondered if this was a medical questionnaire or *Cosmo* quiz.

"Once or twice a week?" he offered.

"Less. You've been sick. Then I got my period."

The next question asked if I suffered from depression. There was no option to say "sometimes," "occasionally," or "always," just "yes" or "no." So, yes, I had clinical depression, but not always. I've kept a leash on it. I wanted to write an essay about it right there on the paper.

I didn't want any doctor or tests telling me *it's not going to be possible.*

. . .

After we handed in our questionnaires, we went to the doctor's office. The impressive letters and words next to Dr. A's name made us want to trust him: MBBS, FACOG, FRCSC, Medical Director, Assistant Professor at McMaster University. Dr. A told me I was healthy, but my egg quality was probably not good. The graph and charts for situations like ours showed the arrows pointing down.

What would I do if he said my egg reserve was empty? He told us we may have other options to discuss later. I asked him about taking Clomid, a drug that helps induce ovulation, but he said we shouldn't waste money until we got our results.

Dr. A took us to the nurse to explain the tests. She drew two vials of blood to see when I was ovulating. I booked the anti-Müllerian hormone test, a blood test that let them know if there are any quality fertile eggs in my mommy tank. The Ontario Health Insurance Plan wouldn't cover the seventy-five-dollar cost, and when Ed paid, I felt a lump in my throat.

When we drove home, Ed asked me if I noticed that part of Dr. A's pointer finger was missing. I remembered that the funeral director who handled my mother's funeral only had half a thumb.

. . .

Lori and I had been texting each other about our fertility tests. She said to make sure my bladder was full for the sonohysterogram because they needed to get a good look at my uterus. I had to drink two bottles of water one hour before the appointment. On the way to the clinic, there was traffic and I was late. I started yelling at the other cars, but really it was my bladder yelling.

When I got to the clinic I had to go to the bathroom so badly that I began pacing around the room and reading thank-you cards from new moms to distract myself. The technician came up to see how I was. She said I could pee, but only for five seconds. In the bathroom, I swear I heard a choir singing the "Hallelujah Chorus" behind me.

The examination was uncomfortable but bearable. The five-second pee helped, and Dr. A said my uterus looked healthy. I had promised myself that I needed to be honest and realistic no matter what the doctor told me, but this starts giving me hope.

When I told Ed about my appointment, he asks me again about the doctor's screwed-up finger. I told him I couldn't see his hands over my knees. It had been so dark in the room that I wiped myself with a gown instead of tissues and put my socks on backwards. So, no, I hadn't seen his weird finger.

A few days later, we got a call from the clinic receptionist, who told us that if it was appropriate, we were to have intercourse for the next three days. I laughed so hard, thinking it was a pretty good prescription.

. . .

Ed went for a semen analysis and thought out loud that perhaps he couldn't have kids. I realized I hadn't thought about how this would affect him. He always said he'd be okay with one child but would have another if I wanted one.

I remembered that when Avery was born, Ed wrote me a lengthy note that included her full legal name, how much she weighed, and how he'd be late that night because he had to drive to the hospital to see her. He was so happy, proud, and excited.

I wanted that for us, for him, for Avery to have a sibling in our home.

They drew my blood to see if I was pregnant, and I would have to wait a few days for the results. I could've bought another test, but I didn't want to know anything until the clinic confirmed. I didn't have any idea what a body felt like when it was pregnant. I knew I felt emotional, like I could happily cry at any moment. Maybe Hans-Peter would let me know somehow.

I passed a sign on a telephone pole that read *Sinners need a saviour.*

"You're telling me," I said out loud, to no one in particular.

. . .

I'm all in, Baby. I'm in.

I'm sorry about before. I was scared. Even if you don't want to talk, I wanted you to know I've taken prenatal vitamins and avoided sushi for you. You know I love sushi.

The other day, I blurted out at a lunch with work friends that we're trying. Were you embarrassed, Baby? I can be too much sometimes. I've wanted to do my best.

I will love you no matter who you are. No matter how long you take. Just give me the chance.

THE SHAPE OF A THING

Winter in the seventies was my father covering our round faces with Vaseline before we went outside. We would only return when our snowsuits got soaked or it became too dark.

Angie, Tammy, Tommy! my mother would yell from the balcony of our Laval, Québec, apartment. She would throw some of the best sledding parties for the kids in the Chomedey congregation of Jehovah's Witnesses. Tobogganing down Bellerive's hills on our Crazy Carpets and wooden sleds was good Christian fun.

This version of Ma made me the envy of other kids. She was a full-time pioneer minister in the congregation, a contributing member of the community, and a good wife and mother. But when she was twelve, she ran away from home because of the abuse, and had been in and out of delinquent and foster homes as a result. She used to hang out with a bad crowd that told her she was worse than them when she drank.

When my parents met at a party in 1959, Ma was only sixteen, and the two pulled to each other's opposites. Ma said that some bad company she had been entertaining was looking for her and my father saved her by taking her to Montréal.

In Montréal, Ma found the Jehovah's Witnesses, and for a time, motherhood and religion became a distraction that would keep her alcoholism at bay. Ma also met her best friend Virginia door-to-door proselytizing. Virginia had curly black hair and a black mole on her left cheek that we never quite managed to stop staring at. Ma used to say that Virginia was the mother she never had, and she became like a grandma to us, always laughing and smiling. My biological grandmother was alive, but we had only met her once; she was as much a stranger to us as she was to our mother.

Since Virginia was part of our chosen family, both literal and spiritual, we were commanded by the Bible to look after her, a widow "in their tribulation, and to keep oneself without spot from the world" (James 1:27). This meant giving her a lift to one of our assemblies at the Côte Saint-Luc hall. My father had just taken his car through the car wash—he hated the salt that the harsh Québec winter left on his dark-blue Buick—and the doors had frozen shut with us all inside. When Virginia came out to meet us, they would not budge, even as my father pushed as hard as he could. We could not get out, and Virginia could not get in.

My father decided the car window would be the perfect entry point for Virginia, and she grabbed a kitchen chair to stand on, and climbed right in. She was a tall woman wearing a dress, and even though she didn't make it the first few times, she refused to give up. For us three kids sitting in the back seat of the car, it was quite the show, and we could not stop laughing. If only this happened every time we had to go to our meetings, I might not have minded wearing those itchy, confining stockings.

One afternoon when I was nine, Virginia's son Richard ran up to me at recess in a panic, wanting to know where Ma was.

Ma was engaged in the Lord's work, preaching while us kids were at school, like she usually was, most likely somewhere in the area. Richard had never come to my school looking for Ma. I don't know why I didn't see the seriousness of it all.

The news came later that Virginia had had a heart attack and did not recover. She was gone, and there would be no replacement, not ever, Ma said.

After that, Ma drank daily for three years straight. While my father was at work, she would get us kids to buy her beer at the dépanneur. Sometimes, I'd drink the beer or pour it down the sink when she wasn't looking. Ma would disappear for hours, and my father would search the local bars to bring her back home. We made our own lunches and got ourselves ready for school, my older sister stepping into the role that Ma had dropped.

I missed what was left of her, even if it was only slivers.

...

Ma said that she had always wanted a family, and when she had her first baby, my sister, she knew motherhood was for her.

I also knew I wanted children—at least five of them. I was a favourite babysitter for the local kids because I played with them even when I wasn't babysitting. While most girls had Rob Lowe or Shaun Cassidy posters in their high school locker, I posted a picture of the Gerber Baby. I hoped that when I got married and had children, I would walk around the Jehovah's Witness assemblies and show people I could be a typical, regular mom. I thought kids would make me feel whole, that my progeny would love me, that my family would be perfect, and that I would not make the mistakes Ma had made.

What I didn't realize was that being religious most of my life would mean that I would remain a virgin for my fertile years, that I would be too busy preaching and avoiding things like sex, long-term commitments, and marriage.

When I got baptized at seventeen, my last year of high school, I made my vow to Jehovah, kept my word, and continued my record of service to him well into my late thirties. I always believed that God would reward those who had been obedient to Him. That He would gift me a spiritual man and the family I so craved and needed.

"For God is not unrighteous to forget your work and the love you showed for his name, by ministering and continuing to minister to the holy ones" (Heb. 6:10).

By the time Ed and I started trying to have a baby, I had stopped praying and going to meetings, so I knew I'd be a hypocrite if I started again. Like in the movies, people only ask God to help them when in dire straits, and that wasn't going to be me. Now that I had strayed from the flock, I didn't think He wanted to listen to me anymore.

Part of me didn't think I deserved to have a baby anyway.

...

After Ed and I went to the fertility clinic and did their tests, Dr. A tells us that I should be thanking my parents for my good genes (which for me was a first).

Dr. A examines my ovaries and declares them healthy and my fallopian tubes unblocked, and his proclamation changes me. Suddenly, men seem more attractive—their angular jaws, broad shoulders, and intoxicating smell. All the blood-test-timed sexual trysts, and the advice from my husband's ex-girlfriend (who also is trying to conceive), are a cross I am willing to bear.

One night, I dream about a baby tightly wrapping his little fingers around mine and not letting go. I am holding him, he's actually mine, and I'm his. I feel joy. When I wake up I want to cry and laugh simultaneously. Finally! I am getting what I wanted. It's going to come true. Hans-Peter is sending me this meaningful sign.

I am hopeful—beyond hopeful even. This baby fever has hit its crescendo.

Women can have babies in their forties. Didn't I just read a story about a sixty-year-old grandmother having a baby for her daughter? On my mother's side, my grandmother's Catholic womb brought forth seventeen kids: Anne, Alexandra, Joan, Diane, Margaret, Catherine, Scott, Louis, Mikey, Willie, Peter, Danny, Alec, Robert, John, Rose-Marie, and Carl. Gosh, with donor eggs, even Janet Jackson had her son at fifty. It's possible.

After enough testing to satisfy the fertility clinic, they schedule us for *the* appointment, the one where they deliver their findings. When the day arrives, they are running more than an hour behind, and Ed is pissed off. When his anger wears off, he falls asleep on the waiting-room couch. The clinic is empty.

Finally, we hear heels clickety-clacking down the hall and our names are called. Apologies are offered and not entirely accepted. The nurse leads us to Dr. A's office.

"Sorry for the wait."

Ed scowls. Glaring at him, I tell the doctor it's okay.

I am a note taker, so I pull out my little pad to calm myself. The baby dream has to be an omen.

The good news comes first.

"Your husband has three times the normal amount of sperm. They seem to have a low survival rate outside the body, but enough survive."

My husband passes all the proper tests. Now, it's my turn.

"You have a low ovary reserve. I don't need a test to tell me that the quality of the eggs isn't very good. Your thyroid is low too, not for your age, but yes, if you wanted to have a baby."

Yes, I did want to have a baby, but now you say no one is home.

Dr. A continues to tell us about our viable options—one of which is getting a donor egg and seeing if I can physically carry it. That's if I pass the physical and the donor wants to give me their eggs after meeting us. *Blah, blah.*

The dream was not a portent after all.

Dr. A tells us that we can review the brochures at home and puts them within grabbing distance, the space between us getting bigger and bigger. I touch the stock photo of happy couples, glance at the price list for the different procedures, and then place the brochures in my bag. I intend to toss them into the recycling right away.

Dr. A tells us to think it over, to not make any decisions until after the holidays, and to please call. I never do. Now I wonder if it was all a big ruse to get us hooked on the idea, even if the clinic never made promises that any of these tests would result in a baby.

Months later, I found the brochures buried in my T-shirt drawer. A memory of my hope, I guess.

...

I am the last of me. I will never know what our child will look like. It's possible he would have looked like that picture printout the app made, the one that combined a photo of me and a photo of Ed and showed us a rendering of our baby. I haven't gotten rid of that picture printout, the one of the baby that has Ed's ears and my eyes.

After our appointment, we go for food at The Burger's Priest, a fast-food restaurant founded by someone who attended seminary school with plans of becoming a priest, and the Scripture on the wall is the Apostle John declaring Jesus to be the Son of God.

I eat my burger and wonder if God is punishing me for everything I've done wrong, for not asking for forgiveness of my sins. I wonder if I wasted my life because I thought I was serving Him and was doing His will, which seems rather pretentious now that I think about it.

...

One of my friends gets pregnant shortly after Ed and I have our last appointment at the fertility clinic. She says that she was afraid to tell me because she didn't want to rub it in my face. I let her know that it's okay, that I am happy for her. She says she was born to do this; she knows it. (Ah, Ma's mantra.) She thinks it might sound hokey, but she loves this baby already, and she cannot explain it.

My friend is experiencing health issues with her pregnancy. She may have gestational diabetes. Her iron is low, and her energy is dissipating. She realizes her body will not go back to the way it was. She says I should be happy that my vagina will still be intact. She says my breasts will not droop, I won't have to take time off from my career, and I can sleep in like a teenager on Saturday mornings for the rest of my life.

I do not know what to do with this sorrow, so I try putting it up on a shelf to deal with later. I wait for a good time to grieve. I should be grateful for everything that I have right now.

I listen to sad songs repeatedly. I cry in the shower.

Maybe the people asking me at work whether or not I am okay are just a coincidence. Maybe I am just tired from life, maybe my iron is also low, or work is just exhausting on a good day. I've seen what depression looks like, and it's nothing like this. It was me sixteen years ago. Anxious, not showering, sleeping all day, taking Paxil. It was hospitalization.

Surely, depression isn't me making appointments to meet with my therapist, who I haven't seen since last year. It can't be me telling Ed that I need meds again to turn the volume down a little and him saying he knew something was wrong after we got the verdict in the doctor's office, that I have not been interested in sex or the gym, and that he thinks deep down I may have known that I am more than a little depressed, that I have been in denial.

When I send my story to my former therapist, she writes, *I too grieve not getting a chance to see a Mini-Tamara in the world*. Oof.

Ed wants to know what happened, how this came on. I realized I have been holding back and have not been honest with how I was feeling.

"Slowly. Then suddenly," I tell him.

He buys me ice cream and teddy-bear graham cracker cookies and asks me to tell him how he can help, and he will.

I tell him to buy me a baby.

"You can be one of those depressed writers and write your bestseller," he says.

I tell him those depressed writers kill themselves.

"That's not funny," he says.

...

I call my old friend Robin. I haven't talked to her for two years and sixty-eight days. I stopped talking to her the night before I got married to Ed, when she told me I had chosen a way without God and that she would pray for me.

I tell Robin I don't want to die, but I don't exactly want to get dressed, either. She tells me the void is there because I no longer have a good relationship with Jehovah. I say I still had sadness when I was in our religion, but I don't want to get into an argument with her because I just needed to hear her voice. She already knows my backstory, and she helps me talk it out.

I watch the seconds tick by. I tell her. I tell her all of it.

I remember Ma singing the Irish lullaby "Too-Ra-Loo-Ra-Loo-Ral" and rubbing my back when I was sick. Ma was always tender to us kids when we were in a feverish haze. The lullaby would be the last thing I heard before I fell asleep.

You'd think I'd have forgotten that by now, but I can still hear her voice.

DADDY DOESN'T KNOW

You hate the tea in the plastic mugs. No sugar in the world will make it better. I know you have tried.

You see how quickly nothing turns into something here. No one can be trusted with knives, razors, or even pills. Patrick snapped like a twig in group just because a nurse asked him how something made him feel. You have seen the scars on Elizabeth's neck and wrists—at least, you think her name is Elizabeth. No one wears name tags here, and you forget everyone's name half the time.

So, who cares about the tea?

Avril paints you a card that says *Thank God for You*. She points her stupid finger in your face, looks at you with watery eyes, and tells you that you're crazy. It hurts your feelings, and you say nope, she is the crazy one. Avril said she lost her temper with her nephew, which is why she is in the hospital with you. She's been painting her white shaggy slippers red, and now they're leaving paint streaks down the hall. You wipe it up behind her.

You and Avril get a tongue-lashing when you take wheelchairs into the parking lot. When Avril falls asleep on the picnic table outside, you tell the nurses her meds must be upped too high because she's drooling in her sleep again. Maybe they upped her drugs because she almost started a riot at breakfast by yelling and agitating everyone.

You pray that you will not see Avril again after this.

You'll be coded as 296.20, major depressive disorder. After you see your doctor, a nurse, the intake coordinator, and a psychiatrist the verdict is suicide watch. That sounds like the beginning of some sad joke. You wonder if this is a "scared straight" tactic or an emergency-room interview process error.

Did you maybe laugh a little too much at the nurse's question about whether or not you were hearing voices?

. . .

Spring is when Ma died. It may have also been spring when you tried telling your doctor about your depths of sadness. You were getting worse with your words. She gave you Paxil for anxiety. You called the employee support line. You were stressed from work, and you weren't sleeping much. You don't remember what a good night's sleep looks like anymore. You would work evenings and weekends to fill the time, but you couldn't run away from yourself.

You were on sick leave from work for a week. The same week, you moved into the basement of Robin's house. You still haven't unpacked. You chatted with Robin on the basement stairs in the early hours and let it slip that you tried to hang yourself. She freaked out. You felt silly. She wanted you to show her the marks, so you pulled your long brown hair back as if you were sporting a hickey, and wondered why you had to prove it. You always were a bad liar anyway.

Robin says the kids could have found you, and you ask her if she thinks you are a sick fuck. Your depression isn't even a depression anymore. It's beyond that.

. . .

"You couldn't even hang yourself right."

Patrick says this after you tell him the yellow rope didn't hold. You've been taking walks with him around the hospital and giving him cookies after you overhear him saying he's stressed about money. He says he probably shouldn't tell you how to tie a knot, but he does anyway.

You don't know if it's the Paxil or the Ativan, but you can't remember shit. You only realize it's your birthday because you get a special placemat, and the other patients are mad they didn't get one too.

Your memory used to be good. You remember that eighteen years ago, you celebrated your fourteenth birthday with your mother, who had been hospitalized in the Jewish General's psych ward. You remember your baby brother coming home from the hospital when you were only two, you and your sister in the back of Daddy's Buick. You remember being mad, so mad you didn't talk to Ma for two weeks.

Your doctor looks at your file and asks why it doesn't say you're a Jehovah's Witness. You tell her that you do not want to bring shame to your religion. She looks puzzled. You want to tell her that God disapproves of suicide, that it's an unforgivable sin, but you're afraid she'll think you're one of those religious nutjobs, so you say nothing.

. . .

Now that you've settled in a little, you like it at the hospital. Your days are simpler than they used to be. You wake up for breakfast, do crafts, go to group, and talk to the psychiatrist with the big wooden desk covered in papers. Expectations are minimal.

Outside of this place, the demands are insatiable. If you leave, you will have to take responsibility for what you have done. You will feel the need to explain that the world would be a better place without you and that no one would ever have to worry about you again. It wasn't anyone's fault that they couldn't see the darkness in you, that it felt like you had a woolly mammoth in your head.

When it's your turn on the wall phone, you call friends and tell them you're fine, but you never call Daddy. You don't want to have to say to him that you went crazy just like Ma. Ma screaming out the front door of your apartment that everyone is out to get her. Ma writing in her green New World Translation Bible and on the floor tiles things like *They're trying to kill me* and *I love Dr. H.* Ma being sent up to the hard-case floor.

Ma was receiving shock therapy, and you imagined her strapped in bed, just like Frankenstein's monster. You have a memory of seeing the red burn marks on her temples. Her face was puffy, and she reminded you a little of the mother you remembered, but you were not so sure because she hadn't been your mother for such a long time.

. . .

You end up staying at the hospital for fifteen days, and you never go back. You fax the hospital eighteen years later to get your records because you want to see who you were back then because you can't seem to remember.

The records never come.

CATALOGUING GRIEF

I am not the first woman to hear she cannot have a baby and won't be the last, but I don't know how to hold this knowledge and function now that my body has betrayed me. I don't know what my grief will look like once I let it out. Will it allow me to be the same person before I thought, *Yes, I can be a mother. I will not be my mother. I will not make her mistakes. I will protect my children no matter what.*

There was a brief period of my life when I didn't want to be a mother. I was depressed and thought it would be terrible to have a mother like me. I thought having a baby would reveal that no matter how good a Jehovah's Witness I had been, even though I had kept my virginity for thirty-nine years, it would be so apparent that I was a fake. I thought that having a baby would reveal everything I hated about myself.

I would say that I couldn't have a baby with Ed when I was in my late thirties because we weren't married yet, but that is only partly true. I also needed to take some writing courses. I needed to save money. I needed to take a trip. So, I waited because I thought we had plenty of time.

I couldn't have known it may have already been too late.

...

Ed and I share custody of his daughter Avery with Ed's ex, Lori. Lori had been trying to get pregnant around the same time as us and was successful, becoming pregnant with twins.

Then she lost them—the first died in utero at twelve weeks and the second was stillborn three months later.

I know that Lori's story is not my story, and I feel guilty when I am depressed about it. I have not carried twins only to lose one and then the other. It is not *my* stillborn baby that she has posted a picture of on Facebook for everyone to see and comment on.

I listen to Lori when she calls me to ask if Ed is still mad that she took Avery to see her stillborn brother. I listen and try not to judge. I tell her that Ed is upset because Avery is eight and he thinks she's too young to see something like that, but I cannot tell her what I think. It is not that simple in these relationships.

If I did tell her how I was feeling I would say that I was angry and sad all at the same time. I would tell her that her actions brought up feelings of not having a mother who would protect me no matter what.

I wonder why it's okay for me to bathe Avery, feed her, kiss her boo-boos, and drive her to swim lessons, but I don't get to share my input on something like this. Instead, I listen while Lori talks to me for twenty minutes about how it all happened, how she had to take medicine to deliver her son. How the whole family was there, and how Avery was so mature about it.

I know that I was not ready at twenty to see my mother's body, so I wonder if Avery was really prepared to see her brother's.

Ed is livid. They had already agreed that Lori would not take Avery to see the baby, and Lori's doctor had said a picture would be good enough. Instead, Lori pulled Avery out of school for the day and called Ed after the fact. He is screaming on the phone, but not at me, and I am trying to calm him down, playing the middle-child role again.

After Ed takes Avery for dinner, he stews but doesn't call Lori. She sends him an angry text saying how dare he, that he is being so insensitive. She tells him not to call the house for a while. He feels betrayed. He says that they had an agreement and he does not want his daughter traumatized. He is just trying to be a good dad, and she should not punish him for looking out for his daughter.

She says that Avery would have been traumatized anyway.

...

Lori is teary when she opens the box of her lost baby's mementos. She shows me prints of his feet, his tiny hands, and, oh—a drop of his blood is also on the paper. There is a blue knit cap too big for his little head. She gets Avery to show me the pictures of her holding her baby brother.

This is a catalogue of her grief, so sweet and horrible at the same time. I feel things in my chest, and my eyes are tearing up. I want to say, *Please do not show me. I do not want to see it. I cannot see it. I refuse to see it.*

Lori explains how her son's skin was all wrinkly, how she had to pull it back on his head, and how she could feel his brain swishing around. She tells me he had fingers, toenails, and his dad's belly. She tells me how Avery wanted to hold him and not let him go.

She mentions the name of the delivery doctor, and I remember he was the same one I would have been referred to if I got pregnant.

Lori keeps talking about how her twins are both angels in heaven now, which seems to comfort her. I used to believe in God and all His promises, that He would remember those who had died and that they would rise up in paradise when the resurrection came. My faith is not what it was, and I no longer know what will happen when we die. I wish that I still had some of that faith. Maybe then I could better hold this together. I would have a net to fall into, the support of some great power above that has a purpose and reasons for all of this.

Standing there with Lori, I know that I need to leave, that Avery and I must escape. But how can I turn away from grief like this?

. . .

On the ride to her swimming lesson, Avery asks me from the back seat if Daddy is still mad at Mommy.

"Not really," I say. "Sometimes, people say things to each other because they're upset, but they can still care about each other. We are all your parents, and we want the best for you. Do you fight with your friends sometimes?"

She nods.

"Does that mean you don't like them anymore?"

"No," she says.

I glance at her in the rear-view mirror.

"See? Sometimes misunderstandings happen, honey."

. . .

After bedtime, Avery cries while hugging her stuffed froggy. I hold her and tell her to come with me to the living room, that she should not stay alone in her bedroom when she's upset, that it's okay to come out and tell us how she is feeling. I ask her if she wants to sleep with Daddy and me tonight.

When she was little, Avery called me Mama. At first, I would correct her. "I am just like a mommy, but you have a mommy," I would say. So she started calling me Tammy.

I ask her if she wants to talk about it, or maybe her frog has something to say, but she says no. We bring her to our bed, and her dad asks her if she wants to talk to someone else about this, and she says yes. My friends have been saying she may need a child psychiatrist, and I am worried.

Ed tells Avery that sometimes Tammy talks to someone, and it helps. She looks at me, and I nod my head.

...

Avery has a sore throat and cough, so I keep her home from school to ensure that it is not her tonsils, which get inflamed from time to time. I call to make an appointment with her family doctor, Dr. Hood, and Ed tells me to ask about a referral for a psychiatrist while I'm there.

Dr. Hood thinks that it's too early to take Avery to counselling. He tells her that her baby brother wasn't in pain; he just never woke up. He tells her she doesn't have to worry that this will happen to her.

Avery does not know that we tried to have a baby. She wanted to give us one of the twins when she learned that was what her mom was having. This little girl loves me but did not come out of my womb. It is hard for me to reconcile this sometimes. My friends tell me that I am her mom. I do everything a mom does, and she looks at me like a mom. Am I a mother only if a baby comes out of my body?

Avery asks why her father and I don't have a kid together. I told her I wanted kids for so long, but I wanted to wait until I got married, that I was afraid I'd be a terrible mom.

She tells me I am a good mom, and I swear I can hear my heart exploding.

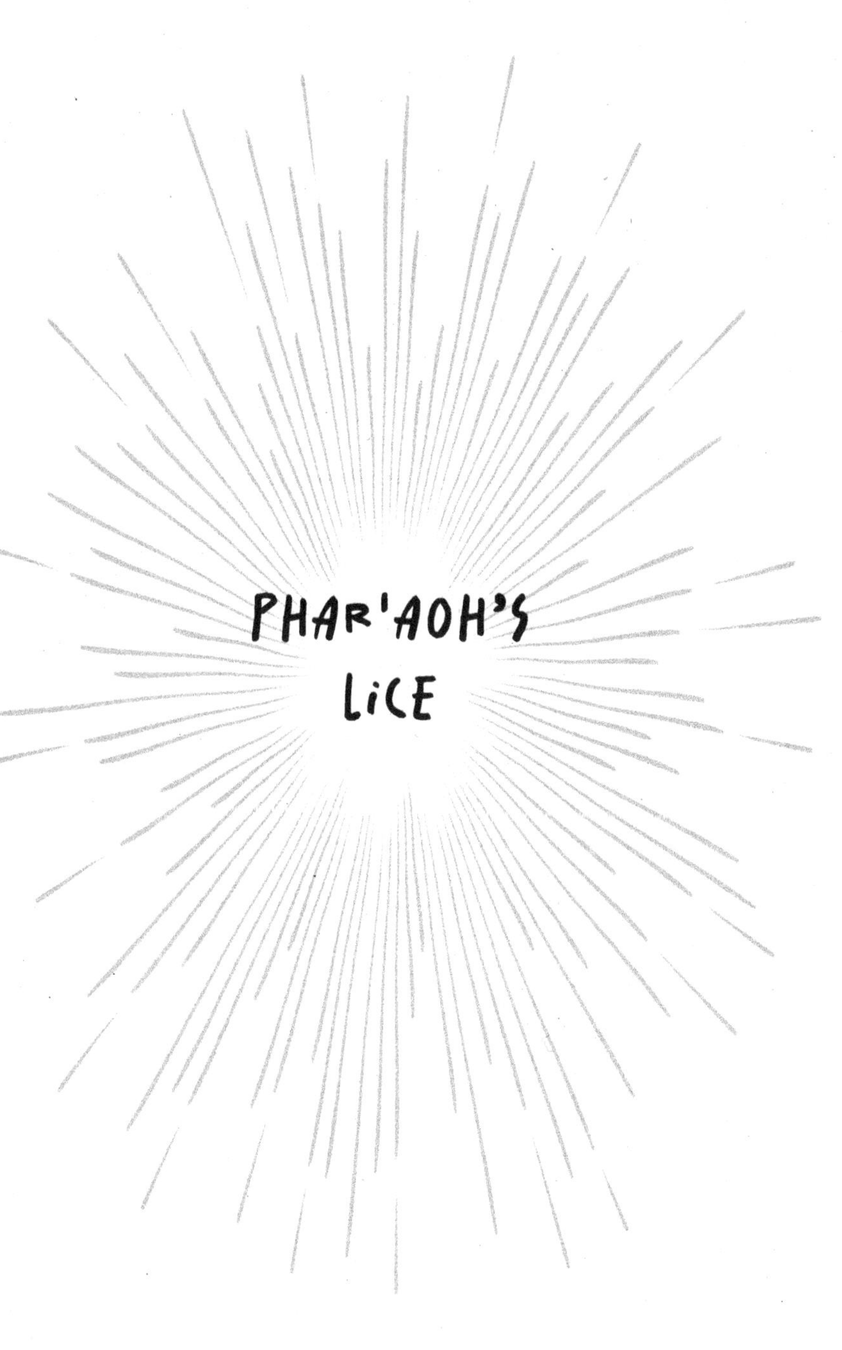

PHAR'AOH'S LiCE

My sister, Angie, got goddamn lice from school when she was eleven. Ma warned us not to play with her, but there's nowhere to go in a puny two-and-a-half-bedroom apartment.

My father cut my sister's long black locks into a boy-cut tout de suite. Our temporary hair salon consisted of a pair of sharp bathroom scissors and a round faded-blue pail with a crack that pinched our bums.

"It took me so long to get rid of the pests!" my dad tells me of this memory.

I wonder out loud why I never got lice, and he laughs and reminds me that I did. (How strange to put faith in his recollection of events because I can't trust my own.)

At the time of the lice outbreak, Ma was otherwise engaged with her bottle, having lost Virginia, her upgraded mother replacement.

Ma had once been charismatic, the life of any party, and with his fabulous hair and karate moves, my dad caught her eye. Ma was the love he never got over, even after the divorce. Even after she died. My dad and I are not close in the ways you'd imagine, but he is the conduit for Ma's stories now that she is gone, and I am searching for the answers only he knows.

This unpeeling is slow, patient work.

. . .

"And the LORD said... Stretch out thy rod, and smite the dust of the land, that it may become lice throughout all the land of Egypt... When Aaron stretched out his hand with the rod and struck the dust of the ground, lice came upon men and animals. All the dust throughout the land of Egypt became lice" (Exod. 8:16–17).

. . .

Lice hide behind ears and at the base of the scalp, places not obvious, areas that someone can easily miss in broad daylight. Look for eggs cleverly camouflaged like sand and specks of dirt; nothing significant. Every strand of hair needs a thorough examination. Lice may masquerade as split ends, but they're not.

First, there are the eggs that have been laid by the adult, close to the base of the scalp. They hatch and then patiently climb up the hair strand with their little claws, becoming a nymph. The nymphs mature into adults, mate, lay eggs, and start the whole cycle again.

Avery is five when Ed and I get the first lice note. There's an outbreak at school. She can't return until there's nothing left of the vermin. We must gird our loins and do battle. It has to be a team effort, or this scenario will repeat itself. (And it does.)

The lice battle comes at a cost. Besides the money for the special shampoo, Avery must stay home from school, meaning we'll all have to take turns using our sick days. My husband handles the laundry, gathering garbage bags full of stuffed animals and clothes and dragging them to the car. He goes to the laundromat down the street for a few hours while I stay in our apartment, treating Avery's hair.

I tell her the story about the cracked blue pail and the sharp scissors and our butts to try to make her laugh, but nothing seems funny right now.

A female louse can lay five to eight eggs daily during her thirty-day life cycle. Her efforts will result in back-breaking work for me, with aching in spots that I didn't think could hurt. My lower back will cry as if it had tear ducts. But no one else can do this work as thoroughly as I can. Ed's hands are too big, and he has been steadily chewing his nails to nubs for years. He tries but doesn't have the patience for this.

It's mentally and physically taxing to deal with lice. It's also gross. I research the shit out of the process, spending nights searching for the signs of a hostile takeover: the nits, the nymphs, the louse. Whatever the name, it's a full-out war.

. . .

Looking behind Avery's ears and at the nape of her neck, I can see specks everywhere. I wonder if I can trust what my eyes see, if I can depend on my intuition. As I work the shampoo through her semi-long blond hair, the lice seem to float, as if they're swimming the breaststroke on the top of her head.

While I work, Avery sits naked in the white bathtub, barely moving, understanding the necessity of staying put. I put a plastic bag on her head to trap the lice and keep the shampoo from dripping into her eyes. After ten minutes, we rinse the shampoo out and watch dead lice rinse away down the drain. I use my desk lamp and comb to go through and closely examine the strands of her hair, dipping the comb repeatedly into alcohol and rubbing it on a paper towel. The hair is slippery, and

I see egg after egg. I can't tell if it's real or my imagination as I methodically comb, comb, comb.

When we finish up, Avery sits on a cushion in the living room watching television, her eyes staring straight ahead. She doesn't say a word, not even a peep.

...

People think lice jump from head to head, but really they crawl to get where they want to go and are pretty fast—9.5 cm per minute. Lice hide in hats, headbands, bedding, hairbrushes, and clothing, and girls appear to attract them more often because their hair is generally longer, they tend to play together in closer proximity, and they are more likely to share their personal items. Lice are said to dislike testosterone, but there's no real proof of this.

Short or long hair, lice like it all. They're looking for a live body pumping blood. Leviticus 17:14 says, "For the life of every sort of flesh is its blood." For lice, your blood gives them the means to feed them and their family.

My husband shaves his head. I wish it were that easy for me. While I threaten to shave my own, I don't. I can't. I'm too much of a chickenshit.

...

Even with all the precautions I take, I get lice from Avery. One day at work, while scratching my head, a louse falls onto my desk, and I freak out.

Why would God create such a thing?

These unwelcome thoughts are something I haven't had in some time. In therapy, I tell my therapist that I don't consider myself spiritual anymore because I no longer subscribe to a particular religion. She says just because I am not religious doesn't mean I'm not spiritual. She says she knows that talking about my former faith is so loaded for me. It is hard to talk about who I was and who I am becoming, with or without a higher power.

My therapist encourages me to listen to a podcast called *Tapestry*. It's for seekers, searchers, and wanderers. Is that me? Do wanderers go in circles? I write the name of the podcast carefully in my notebook. I am a perpetual note taker, a skill I picked up from my JW learnings. My life has been organized into clearly defined routines of study, meetings, and preaching.

It is difficult for me to discuss God or religion without the bias of my former faith. I don't know who I am anymore without religion. Is what I believe even mine? If I lost my memory, would I choose to be a Jehovah's Witness again? Would I be a God-fearing moral person and follow the Bible's rules? I was sure of who I was back then, believing in God's Kingdom and the prophecies. It didn't bother me that people didn't listen to what we had to say at their doors. Our responsibility was to share the good news of God's Kingdom; it was up to others to decide for themselves. Because we were just messengers. They were rejecting Him—not us.

Hadn't Jesus and his apostles been ignored, persecuted, and murdered on behalf of his name? We weren't dragged away from the garden of Gethsemane, betrayed, then put up on a stake to die. We were getting off easy if all we got was a few doors slammed in our faces. We had a purpose.

What am I without religion? What am I without the safety of us?

(I realize this sounds like cult talk as I write it.)

...

Lice can't live without a host after twenty-four hours. Severe cold or severe heat will kill them.

Mummies had lice.

There are over 5000 species of lice, and they can hold their breath for up to an hour, sometimes more.

Eggs can camouflage to match your hair colour.

Our heads get itchy because we're allergic to their bites.

...

When another lice note comes home from school, I swear the usual swear words.

People keep saying it is weird to hear me swear. They're used to me being the Bible-toting, rules-following religious one, always in control.

It's not that I never used to swear at all, it's just that I would ask for forgiveness when I did so. What do I miss about being a Witness, believing and praying to God? Being forgiven? Does God ignore those who leave Him? Does He miss me?

I don't have the answers. At least, not the answers I'm ready to face.

...

The instructions on the box tell me to repeat the lice treatment process in seven to ten days, about the same amount of time it took God to create the heavens and the earth. These connections often come up for me without invitation. If you're curious, that results from about thirty-six years of training.

I don't have as many friends to discuss scripture with now that I've abandoned the faith. I don't want to go all anti-religious or apostate, but I wish there was a space where I wouldn't feel so weird now that I've left the Witnesses. I never thought I'd miss chatting about the Bible, doctrine, or our assembly discussions, but I do.

Let's imagine I found a safe place to talk about God. I would ask why after the lice, it would take seven more plagues for Phar'aoh to let the Israelites go, but at the same time I know that God had already predicted "... Phar'aoh's heart to become obstinate, and I will multiply my signs and my miracles in the land of Egypt" (Exod. 7:3). Phar'aoh thought himself not only like a god but equal to God himself, which I imagine pissed Jehovah off.

Jehovah would win. He always does.

If I had a safe space to talk about God, I would notice that, curiously, in this chapter *heart* is mentioned five times, that it would be the final plague Jehovah performs, the death of Phar'aoh's first-born son, that would allow him to finally release the Israelites from their servitude.

If I had a safe space to talk about God I would marvel at Phar'aoh's heart and mind, wonder what made him chase after the Israelites and war with God Almighty. How he could've backed down, but he didn't. It may have been his grief. Perhaps it wasn't easy for Phar'aoh to turn his back on his upbringing, gods, and teachings from infancy. He saw literal miracles from above, a power beyond comprehension, and chose instead to die in the Red Sea with his armies.

For a moment, I empathize with Phar'aoh's grief, see the loss of everything I knew, and realize that out of that I can do things I hadn't imagined.

Maybe these are just stories meant to entertain. Maybe my faith had been a mother's gift to her daughter, a keepsake to hold on to. Still, I wonder what exactly I keep chasing and when I will finally feel free.

. . .

I have repeated the process as the box instructed, down to the letter. The days, the thoroughness. I have checked Avery diligently. I have done what I could. Over and under, fingers and combs, a lamp used to scour her little head. She, as always, sits still.

Soon, Avery will forget all this. Maybe I will too.

ARE YOU THERE, GOD? IT'S ME, TALKING TO MARY KARR

Dear Mary,

I want "Stay Lit" tattooed on my body.

You wrote that inscription for me when we met at a creative non-fiction conference. You were the keynote. I have been writing since 2011, having recently switched gears from fiction to non-fiction. When my teacher Ayelet Tsabari introduced me to your work, I felt a kinship. The way you write and how you sound when you're talking, your humour in the darkest stories. What you went through with your parents and your dysfunctional childhood were things I related to and wrote about—a lot. While you got into drugs and drinking, I just picked up religion full on.

When we met, I didn't have the guts to mention the typed-up letter I sent you about how you changed the way I view faith. I considered writing the letter in cursive, but I didn't want to subject you to my serial-killer chicken scratch. Most times, I can't even read it myself. I did not inherit Ma's beautiful handwriting—all big loops and ball gowns.

I'd like to think if I had told you about the letter, it would have been as good a moment as when that fan said reading your book was like coming home, and you got off the stage to comfort her. My friend who came with me to your keynote said we don't want to be *that* person. We don't. To be so vulnerable in the moment is a skill I fight, but I did think about mentioning this letter. As much as I believe I am not *that person*, I am *that person* inside.

I just wanted to let you know that *Lit* hit me straight in whatever heart I have left.

. . .

Your mother was an artist. Mine was a poet, like you. What kind of poet, it's hard to say. We only have a few lines left that my brother found after she drowned in 1987. Everything else ended up in a landfill. I was the one who dragged her poetry in boxes to the curb. I'm undecided about whether I can forgive myself for that.

When I read *Lit*, so many childhood memories of Ma came back. Your words reminded me that it's okay to revisit things because no one can hurt me now.

. . .

Religion and spirituality have been a struggle for me lately. I so desperately want to be secure knowing it's not on me to have the answers, that someone will tell me why the world is the way it is, that God will fix things and there are reasons beyond this realm.

Ma must have wanted to make a different life for her children, give them a community that was safe, where they would be protected and cared for. It's curious what a mother's love will make her do to keep a child from certain types of hell.

I was baptized *twice*—first as a Catholic and later as a Jehovah's Witness. The first—a sprinkling by John Bobinas—took place in 1967 at St. Patrick's Basilica, founded in 1947, downtown Montréal. The second was full-on immersion in an Assembly Hall of Jehovah's Witnesses in the same city. I was seventeen and don't remember Ma being there, but she must've come.

Before Ma converted to the Jehovah's Witnesses, we used to celebrate Christmas and birthdays—all that heathen stuff. Then she got religion in a not-joking-around-anymore-hardcore-serious-type way. She'd heard the Jehovah's Witnesses on the radio around the time my little bro came on the scene, so when the sisters showed up at our apartment door with *The Watchtower* and *Awake!* she took it as a sign from the Almighty.

When I was in half-day kindergarten it was all gerbils, hot-dog days, Barbies, cookies, and juice, but grade 1 meant whole days away from Ma in a strict get-down-to-business kind of way. I gotta say I took solace in having Jehovah around then. Before Him I was scared a lot of the time, a real crybaby, so having access to God in every moment, especially when I was away from Ma, really helped.

I would get math all jumbled in my brain. I would get scolded for chatting. I would fret about the punishment that would come when Ma found out I got put into the corner. But Jehovah blessed those who followed His rules, and no follower was too little to be a good worshipper. Once, I was so upset that I told my teacher Mrs. Cohen it would help me if I could go into the hall and pray to Jehovah. She let me go and get in a good old chat with Him just outside our classroom door.

Thanks to Ma, I was real little when I started being a big old believer.

My children's book *From Paradise Lost to Paradise Regained* had pictures of unbelievers, naysayers, and do-nothings destroyed for not choosing Jehovah's side at Armageddon. Those images made it into my nightmares. Buildings collapsing. People running, screaming, and falling into pits where earthquakes had split open the ground.

My sister tells me these prophecies still cross her mind from time to time. She doesn't go to the Kingdom Hall anymore, but the pull of the past life still lingers.

. . .

When I was nine, Ma took me on the train to visit her foster mom in Toronto while my brother and sister stayed at home. My father must have thought she'd drink less if one of us was with her. I remember she left me alone in my seat on the train for what felt like hours.

Ma used to send us to the store to get her beer and cigarettes. After school, day after day, we would find her sitting at our kitchen table, sipping her Brador stubbies and listening to the same records on repeat. I still feel triggered when I hear Supertramp, Jessi Colter, Kenny Rogers, or Tom Jones.

My dad didn't convert. He studied the Bible with the elders in the congregation and cooked for the brothers and sisters, but he didn't become a Jehovah's Witness. Years later, he would tell me that he was *too bad to change*, but that being a Witness was good for us kids. He tried to pay the bills but wasn't home much, preferring to play basketball or hang out with his friends in Chinatown.

He also had lots of affairs, according to the phone bills my mother found.

There'd be full-on fights when my mom and dad were home together. When he was really mad, he'd switch to Cantonese mid-argument. Eventually, he didn't want to be a husband or a father, so he checked out for good.

Ma went on welfare when she and my dad split. Some lady came to our digs and checked the box that said, *yeah, sure, they're poor,* and that was that.

. . .

I know all this Jehovah's Witness stuff sounds like a bunch of hooey, but I wouldn't be here now without Jehovah or the brothers and sisters in the congregation. Everyone viewed us kids as orphans and took care of us.

Even though my home life was less than ideal when I lived in it, I wasn't wondering what would happen next. I was just trying to get through the day. Only now do I dare to ask my brother and sister about their versions of what happened.

"Remember when Mummy was up all night making popovers, and then she didn't get up in the morning?" my sister would ask, and suddenly I'm fourteen again.

Mary, as a writer and an alcoholic and believer, you helped me understand Ma's ways. I hated her because of the drink. She got sober through Alcoholics Anonymous, and even though I sat through a baker's dozen of her speaker talks, I never really listened. When you said your mother's sobriety was a gift, it was something I wish I realized when my own mother was alive.

My brother and sister and I went to Alateen while Ma went to the meetings, and we were supposed to take turns talking about our problems. I had heard the teaching that the devil is the ruler of Christendom, so being in those church meetings creeped me out. In Kingdom Halls, there are no icons, no robes, and there was definitely no Jesus hanging around on a cross, looking like he'd also like to be anywhere but staring down on us sorry sacks, week in and week out.

At the Kingdom Hall things made sense. Jehovah's congregation made me feel safe and cared for, and being a part of the brothers and sisters worldwide, commissioned to preach about his name, gave me a job that would keep me busy for a lifetime. I was a real keener when it came to pleasing others, especially Jehovah. I could count on His rules and knew that if I stuck to His written word, I would have an entry into His "book of remembrance."

In my teens, I'd get into religious debates and offer my friends Bible studies because I didn't want them dead at Armageddon. I got rid of any records that seemed unchristian, and refused to watch movies that contained sex, drugs, or violence. I didn't lie, stand for the national anthem, or celebrate holidays. I didn't date boys until I was a marriageable age, and I didn't want much to do with Ma when she'd veered off the path. There were many rules to follow, and I was happy to comply because the faith reminded me of a time when our family had been (mostly) happy, united, and stable.

When I was seventeen and decided to dedicate my life completely to Jehovah, I had to study the *Organized to Accomplish Our Ministry* book with the elders to see if I was ready for baptism. I had to be a good Christian example and an active preacher of the good news. Once the elders approved, I got baptized at the next assembly at the Côte Saint-Luc Assembly Hall of Jehovah's Witnesses, where I took vows in public before Jehovah and my fellow Witnesses. (This was the biggest deal.)

I was one of four that day, sitting in the first few rows. We loudly responded to the two questions asked of us.

Have you repented of your sins, dedicated yourself to Jehovah, and accepted His way of salvation through Jesus Christ?

YES!

Do you understand that your baptism identifies you as one of Jehovah's Witnesses in association with Jehovah's organization?

YES!

"For with the heart one exercises faith for righteousness, but with the mouth one makes public declaration for salvation" (Rom. 10:10).

After this affirmation of faith, we were each baptized individually, an elder in a short-sleeved, white T-shirt and swim trunks fully submerging us in an unassuming beige wading pool. It was small, not meant for swimming, with a set of stairs and a railing leading down into it.

The water was noticeably chilly. When I was under, I expected to feel something other than just the cold. It felt like I was in slow motion under the water, but there were no apparent signs of the holy spirit.

My non-religious father came to see the momentous event but missed my actual dunking. He is perpetually late but still made the effort. Ma was there to commemorate this important milestone but, of course, at that point hadn't been coming to the meetings on the regular.

. . .

I was taught that Jehovah came first and family second and was determined to serve as a faithful servant. It would only be later, when I was in my late thirties, that I would blame Jehovah for my bad relationship with Ma. I left Jehovah much like my dad left us—slowly at first, and then deliberately. I thought I'd return to the Witnesses after a pause but couldn't. I used to pray several times a day—sometimes, I even fell asleep in prayer—but eventually stopped talking to Jehovah altogether.

In 2006, my new therapist told me she couldn't promise that I would still be a Jehovah's Witness at the end of our work together. At the time, I scoffed at the idea—she didn't know me or my faith. I was a rock. Besides, I wasn't coming to her to figure out anything about being a Witness. That part was helping me. It was my self-esteem, the drinking, my childhood, and my parents I needed help with—at least I thought it was. The reality was I was working a lot, hardly going to meetings, and feeling guilty.

They call these kinds of JWs "PIMO"—physically in, mentally out.

If I hadn't isolated myself from Jehovah's congregation, the truth of His word, things might have been different. I was now a disappointment to everyone. But you really can't go back once you get far away from a thing, no matter how familiar it once was.

...

In 1999, after being on stress leave from work, a suicide attempt put me in the hospital. I was prescribed Paxil and Ativan, and I felt like a failure. I got put into what you called the "nervous hospital." (Your mother, my Ma, you, and I all have that in common.)

I was still a Jehovah's Witness then, although I can't remember the content of my prayers.

At the time, I honestly thought the world would be a better place without me, and Jehovah standing right in front of me couldn't have convinced me otherwise. That was when I started changing, and the change altered my relationship with the God and Father I knew. I just thought it would be easier to be religion-free.

I didn't run off to become a stripper, or a drug addict, or get covered in tattoos like some ex-religious girls do. And honestly, even if I did all those things, I think being judgmental is the most un-Christ-like thing of all.

It was hard to believe that I was, at one time, a faithful, dress-wearing, proselytizing Jehovah's Witness, and then I threw in the towel.

That's it. I'm done.

...

Recently, I felt called to go to Montréal, my hometown. I wanted to see Saint Patrick's, the church my parents took me to as an infant.

I woke up several times early the morning I went, afraid I'd miss Mass. I got lost trying to find the 226-foot-tall building, and when I finally saw it, my heart was beating so fast, and the bells were chiming, and I realized it'd taken two therapists and eleven years to find my feelings.

When I was there I paid four dollars to light a candle for Ma. (She's never far from my thoughts.) They weren't actual candles, but battery-operated, and none of them would turn on.

A fine start, I thought.

The sermon was about doubting Thomas, the skeptic, and I finally understood why he needed to feel the imprint of the nails in Jesus's side to believe. I never questioned while in the faith, only when I was outside of it. My therapist used to say that maybe it's not about the answers, perhaps it's about the questions. Now all I have are questions.

I want to go back to the beginning, to where Ma started my spiritual journey for me. She was only twenty-three, probably hopeful, maybe even happy about my future. I wonder what commitment she made that day, trying to start me off right, trying to save my soul.

Mary, thank God you didn't give up on writing *Lit*. You said once that you tossed out the equivalent of four books before you found the right words to write it.

Even though everything appeared to fall apart for me, it's kind of a beautiful mess, isn't it?

Daughter, sister, searcher, believer,
Tamara

NOT A BAD
TOWN IF YOU'RE
NOT IN A CULT

In May 2020, early in the pandemic, a young female humpback whale strayed from the salt water of the St-Lawrence Gulf and was seen swimming in Montréal's Old Port. It is thought she came from The Laurentian Channel, near Tadoussac where the salt water mixes with fresh water. The Groupe de recherche et d'éducation sur le mammifères marins believes she may have been chasing fish and got lost exploring, but no one knows for sure. Montréalers gathered to take pictures and videos of her, and she became a celebrity and a marvel to watch.

Everyone was hoping she'd find her way out naturally, but unfortunately, she died a week later, and Montréalers mourned her loss.

In the summer of 2019, I was supposed to go on a whale-watching tour with Ed, Avery, and my mother-in-law on our way to P.E.I. I hadn't been out east since doing some preaching work in Baddeck, Nova Scotia, when I was twenty-one. We looked forward to seeing the minke, humpback, finback, and North Atlantic right whale.

A month earlier, Lori died suddenly in a head-on collision that was all over the news. Avery, who was twelve at the time, didn't want to cancel the trip. She wanted to see the whales.

I had seen Lori the night before the accident. It wasn't actually our night to have Avery over, according to the custody agreement, so my last words to her were, "Thanks for letting me take your kid." She told me that I was her mom too.

It was the last time I saw her.

When we got to the whale-watching boat, a young girl sat alone at the bow. She explained that the company hadn't gotten its boating licence renewed in time and we wouldn't be able to go out that day. They had emailed us and refunded the deposit, but we had been on the road and hadn't seen the email.

While there were no guarantees that we would see any whales on the tour, we had hoped to have a temporary distraction from grief, at least for Avery's sake. But it wasn't to be.

According to researchers, the stranded young female humpback was the first that had ever been spotted in Montréal. She brought the city happiness during a time when it was challenging to find joy. Everyone had hoped she'd find her way home, even though she was young and inexperienced.

I imagine when people no longer saw her swimming in the Old Port, some thought, *Oh good, she figured it out. She's found her way home.*

. . .

Michael and I stood in Union Station in downtown Toronto—the place of many goodbyes. What I wanted to say to him was *I want to drive you home. I don't want this moment to end.* I wanted to say all the ridiculous proclamations of love and have everything end happily. I mock these kinds of happy-ending stories out loud, but my pathetic heart soaks them up inside.

While I'm at Union Station—looking out, looking in—I know that this moment will always haunt me, all the what-ifs of a different path with Michael. Oh yes, I'm only too aware of Paul's words, "Look out that no one takes you captive by means of the philosophy and empty deception...of the world" (Col. 2:8). Michael was worldly, and I was not. I was a religious Christian woman who wore modest dresses 80 per cent of the time.

What did I know about love at the age of thirty-two? I was past spinster status by Jane Austen standards. I knew only the blow-up of my parents' marriage and the conditional love of my religion. I didn't even love myself.

Michael was a good person, even if he jokingly called himself the Antichrist. He said I could be the designated driver when he'd party. By that he meant I would have to go to his world, but I couldn't entertain that, couldn't imagine the parts of my life that would be missing. Being with him would mean I'd have to walk away from a place and community where I felt I belonged, a place that had saved me from my childhood.

Later, I would find pages and pages of bad poetry about Michael, which would be hard for me to read. Words like *anger*, *pain*, *abandonment*, *yearning*, and *emptiness* fill those pages. In the poems I never name him, but it is clear I hated myself for wanting to be with him. I knew that it was wrong, but I couldn't stop.

We had shared feelings but not a kiss. Oh, but I wanted to.

I will revisit this farewell in Union Station many times over the following days, years, and even decades. But I knew I could not resist him if I went through with driving him home. I would not resist him.

Ghosts aren't the only ones who leave traces of who they were behind.

. . .

One of the stories I have always liked in *My Book of Bible Stories* is "Isaac Gets a Good Wife." I was eleven when the book was published, and I read about how Abraham sent a servant to get his son Isaac a wife. Isaac could not choose a wife from Ca'naan as they didn't serve Jehovah.

In the story, when the servant's camels become thirsty on the journey, he prays to Jehovah that the woman who gets them water will become Isaac's wife. That woman turns out to be Re·bek'ah, and she agrees. When Isaac first sees Re·bek'ah, he falls for her, and theirs is one of the Bible's great love stories.

I wanted that—that one big love. Forget that Isaac and Re·bek'ah's union would become the lineage leading to Jesus Christ.

. . .

To me, Michael was Frederick in *Persuasion.* He was Adam in *Joan of Arcadia*. He was Jordan in *My So-Called Life,* and Conrad in *The Summer I Turned Pretty.*

For so long, I was cemented in a sixteen-year-old version of myself, stuck in the time when Noah dumped me and I didn't know why. What reasons for getting dumped would make sense to a teenage heart? Years later, I would ask him, and he would say he didn't know. I think he knew but didn't want to hurt me.

I came up with the no-kissing rule after Noah so that I would not be emotionally connected to anyone again, and I wasn't until I broke that no-kissing rule for Michael. Michael standing before me at the train station, in the brief window where he could have been mine. But maybe he was never going to be mine.

I thought nothing would happen to you if you dated me, said Michael.

I can't leave my religion for you, I said.

That much was true. I would not be ready to leave for years.

. . .

Michael and I were friends at first. He had a girlfriend when I met him, and, initially, I didn't like him *that way*. We worked together in the mailroom at a credit card company, and that was all. He was a nice guy—decent, kind, fun. He was tall and rugged-looking, with hair shaved close to his head, long sideburns, and blue eyes. He smoked cigarettes but didn't smell like smoke, drove a cool old Lincoln, and wore a leather jacket and Doc Martens. He told me he was a writer and had taken some college business courses.

I knew he was someone who would raise eyebrows in my Kingdom Hall.

I was twenty-three when I first met him, naive in many ways, not understanding what lines could be crossed and uncrossed. I didn't see the harm in hanging out with him while working full-time, and he and his friend Patrick welcomed me in. They taught me about things I didn't know, which was a lot of things.

In some ways, I wanted to be like Michael. I even got my first pair of Doc Martens because of him. I started wearing more black. We were young and hopeful, and we shared our dreams with each other. Patrick even came to one of the Jehovah's Witnesses assemblies with me. I laughed a lot with them both.

I was happy to spend time with people who welcomed me and who didn't want anything in return. I told Michael I was a writer, too, and let him read my work. He even thought one of my poems was about him. (It was written about someone who didn't matter, a nobody. Maybe it was about me, thinking about it now.) I was sad for Michael when he broke up with his girlfriend, but also surprised and thrilled. He said it was a good breakup. He said I was more upset about it than his ex.

Maybe I was worried about myself and my own heart.

...

My friend at work, Micheline, whom I had confided in about Michael, knew all about my feelings. She insisted Michael was not good or right for me. We were too different, she said, and I was to call her whenever I felt weak. She seemed relieved when I told her what had happened at Union Station, reassuring me that this was for the best.

That was debatable.

I had a team on call rallying against the idea of Michael and me. My friend Carrie from Montréal was worried about my spiritual soul, and she had the right to be. I told her in a letter that I thought I was in love with him and wondered how it happened. Had I lost my mind? I knew we couldn't be together.

Crystal was concerned about Michael's "badness" but listened to me endlessly prattling on about him. She, too, was worried about me and wrote encouraging notes telling me to be strong, but I knew it would have to be my decision to let him go.

No one could make me do anything.

...

I turned to look at Michael again after we parted at the train station. I was Lot's wife, turning into a pillar of salt when she looked longingly back at the city of Sod'om. Maybe she had a friend, a pet, a forgotten love. The object of her gaze is omitted from *My Book of Bible Stories*, as is any reaction to her death from her family. There is no mention of her again in the Bible, except as a warning.

I judged myself even as it was happening, hoping for a different end—a curious limbo.

...

On *The Nature of Things*, season 63, episode 6: "Love Hurts: The Science of Heartbreak," host Anthony Morgan speaks with researchers and scientists to discover the biological effects of a broken heart. Morgan says he wants to know "what happens to our hearts and minds and bodies when we go through those kinds of emotional trauma." Later in the show, a biological anthropologist, Dr. Helen Fisher, shares that she has done a brain scan of a "heartbreak candidate" and showed them their lit up nucleus accumbens.

"It's an addiction, whether you're madly in love or heart-broken," she says. "Love hurts, literally and figuratively."

I wasn't surprised. I didn't need a documentary to tell me what a broken heart feels like. I was despondent about Michael. I was torn apart like I was being taxidermized—there was my carefully preserved outside, and only stuffing inside.

After I parted with Michael, I couldn't stand not being busy. I had to schedule every hour, every second. I didn't sleep. I felt sick. I worked too much and felt stressed out. I ate too little and was too skinny. I thought about him obsessively, hoping I'd run into him at work and also hoping I wouldn't. I know I drank too many bottles of Robin's ice wine from the case in her basement. I was channelling Ma in my behaviour.

Since drunkenness is considered one the "works of the flesh" (Gal. 5:19), I focused on the fact that I was being faithful to Jehovah by not running off with Michael.

...

At our meetings, I wondered what it would be like to have Michael come with me, preach with me, have him sit beside me and serve Jehovah. I was only too aware of what the scriptures said: "she is free to be married to whomever she wants, only in the Lord" (1 Cor. 7:39). I couldn't ask Michael to convert. I couldn't be one of *those* sisters that the congregation whispers about, but I wanted to be.

Michael had told me that he loved me, and I knew I was in trouble. We talked about God, religion, and life. He knew how important it all was to me. I wanted him to read my mind and convert without me asking him to.

Maybe we could date, get married, and be happy for eternity. That would be the grand, romantic, sweeping gesture. Perhaps I would care what my congregation thought at first, but if Michael did all of this without me trying to convince him to do it, that this commitment was for Jehovah, then his works would be evidence of his faith since *faith without works is dead* (Jas. 2:26). I prayed to Jehovah that he really would.

Jehovah could see how I was struggling. If he cared for me, something had to give.

After the ice wine ran out, Robin was worried and advised me to talk to Brother Johnson. She knew what could happen if I kept carrying on like this. Brother Johnson counselled me and told me I would continue doing the right thing. I wondered how many other sisters had come to Brother Johnson for advice or to repent. There was nothing for me to repent. Michael and I had never even talked about sex. My actions had not led to physical sin—not yet.

Brother Johnson gave me a script to follow: *You cannot see him again. You cannot be friends.* I appreciated his understanding and empathy. I had heard elders sometimes ask things that would make you blush, but he didn't. He didn't report me as far as I knew, and it felt like he trusted me. He was rooting for me.

Robin's husband couldn't believe Michael and I hadn't been intimate. How could I be so attached if nothing had happened?

For him to ask that question, he couldn't have known me at all.

. . .

In that "Love Hurts" episode, they talked about something called reconsolidation therapy, where, for six sessions, willing participants agreed to take propranolol and talk about their breakup. The memory is there, but at some point, the pain of it is somehow lower because of the drug. It's more like a bad memory, and the feeling associated with it is muted.

Honestly, if I had access to it, I would have chosen to take a drug instead of holding on to the painful memories for as long as I did.

I now believe that Michael was also a contributing factor to my ending up in the hospital. The suppression of my feelings for him drained me in so many ways. I felt like a shell of a person. I had told the nurse that I had not had a long-term romantic relationship for quite some time, and it had troubled me. Even then, I could not admit to myself or them what that relationship had taken from me. It was a prolonged mourning with seemingly no end.

. . .

After I left the hospital, I returned to work and ran into Michael in the hallway. I recognized his walk and immediately knew it was him. He commented that he hadn't seen me in a while, and I offered that I had been in the hospital. He said he was sorry to hear that.

Michael told me that Patrick was leaving the company and that there would be a pub party and we could all meet up at Patrick's first. I agreed to go. I thought I could handle it. What could happen? Michael had a girlfriend now, and in the hospital I may as well have died and been reborn. I was this rock of faith, on meds, and feeling better than I had in years.

We met at Patrick's place, where everyone drank, except for me. I had to have my mental capacity. It was strange to be in this space with Michael, pretending things were fine after all this time and all the things we had said or didn't say. I wasn't over him—I knew that much. I found it hard to breathe, simultaneously feeling invigorated and terrified. I realized it might take more than a hospital stint to get rid of him.

A girl at the party wanted to know who I wanted that night—Michael or Patrick.

"Doesn't Michael have a girlfriend?"

She shrugged off my question.

That night I took a group picture, pretending to commemorate Patrick's departure but only wanting a photo of Michael. I didn't have any since Robin made me throw them all away. At the time, I had thought it was for the best.

Since I was the designated driver, Michael had me drive him to the pub from Patrick's place. I wished we didn't ever have to leave the car. Every moment I was living now would not happen again. It would be final—even more than that night at Union Station.

I had arranged to sleep over at my friend Gwen's in the city so I wouldn't have to drive back to Robin's. It was getting late. I knew if I didn't leave, I would never want to leave. I didn't plan for anything to happen. I had entertained the thought of going to Patrick's that night because Michael was going and I wanted to be where Michael was.

I decided to leave the pub before I gave in. I don't know if I prayed to do this.

A bunch of us were standing around talking, and I asked Michael to walk me to my car. We wandered over and the air felt electric. We weren't standing far apart when I asked him why he hadn't ever tried to kiss me.

I honestly can't remember his answer. Everything stopped. It was tender and short. It was like a fucking movie.

I did what I usually did—I ran away again. I told Michael I had to go. I think I even apologized. I got into the driver's seat and left him in the parking lot, watching me leave.

But I always had to look back. Always.

...

Later, when I heard Michael got married, I was slightly devastated, but what did I think would happen after all this time? Maybe the kiss meant something to him or maybe it meant nothing, but I know part of me was selfish. I had been what people call a tease, even if that is not what I set out to do. I wasn't experienced with boys and existed in a world where barely touching a member of the opposite sex was a thrill. I wasn't thinking straight when it came to Michael.

I wanted him to have a good life, even if it wasn't with me. I don't know if I deserved the same.

. . .

Years later, after I left the Witnesses, I never thought about reaching out to Michael. I had to work on who I was without religion and try to get past a laundry list of things I thought were wrong with me. I hadn't even really mentioned him in therapy. I couldn't. I didn't know if I could have a long-term relationship—I had to figure out how things worked in the real world.

I didn't know if I could be fixed, but my therapist insisted that I wasn't broken. That was news to me, but it helped my mind a little.

Eventually, when I connected with Patrick on LinkedIn, he asked me if I knew Michael had broken his leg while driving his motorcycle. Patrick knew about the kiss and how I felt, had told me after it had happened that Michael was with someone else and that I should have understood that.

I told Patrick that Michael and I weren't in touch. I had seen that he was on Facebook but didn't feel it would be appropriate to reach out. The reality was I didn't need to. I wasn't the same person I was back then—she was long gone. Yes, she had been in love, but she wasn't now.

If there were a scan of her brain, the light where love had been would be gone.

. . .

A two-year-old orca calf—named kʷiisaḥiʔis (Brave Little Hunter) by the Ehattesaht First Nation—was in the news recently. Her pregnant mother had been beached and died despite rescue efforts, and now the calf was stranded in a lagoon near Little Espinosa Inlet near Vancouver Island. The shallow water and low tides left her unable to swim out, and she was without her family, alone, stressed, and grieving, circling near her mother's body. Calves do not usually leave their mothers; they stay with the same pod until adulthood.

Everyone was worried the calf would suffer the same fate as her mother. The longer she stayed trapped, the lower her chances of survival. The community was rooting for her and kept her company, monitoring her health and working together to come up with a plan. The Ehattesaht First Nation, the Nuchatlaht First Nation, Fisheries and Oceans Canada, the Vancouver Aquarium, and many others were involved, everyone trying to be optimistic that the little calf would somehow be rescued or that she'd figure a way out on her own.

Young kʷiisaḥiʔis was learning more every day. She was, however, clearly not ready to get out on her own. She needed to stay a little bit longer. She needed to build up the courage to do what she needed to do.

One night the calf eluded four members from the Ehattesaht First Nation. Rob John, Judea Smith, Victoria Wells, and Ashley John had unsuccessfully tried to coax her out of the lagoon, feeding her sea lion along the way. They could only take her as far as she was willing to go.

A short time later, in the early morning at high tide, the calf headed past the sandbar her mother had died on, swam under the bridge, and headed toward the open waters. She was last seen swimming in the moonlight, free at last.

SAINT, FEARS. FATHERS, ORIGINS: A DIPTYCH

It was unbearably hot and humid the summer I returned to my hometown to see Brother André's heart. Canonized as a saint after his death, Brother André was known as "the miracle man of Montréal," a Catholic layperson who believed in Jesus's ability to heal, and who himself was known for performing thousands of miracles. I went to see him the week before my fifty-first birthday, and the drive without working AC felt like a hell if I ever believed in one.

I had felt called to go to Montréal. My therapist told me that sometimes you have to go backward to go forward, and I needed to see versions of my past self, to witness the old and new and what remained of my faith. I wanted to trace my past by visiting the places that had scared me as a child.

Had I become the type of person hoping to see Jesus in her multi-grain toast?

I took 283 sweaty steps up Mount Royal because the thought of taking the shuttle bus up to St. Joseph's Oratory seemed ridiculous. I marveled at the devotion of those who recited a prayer while crawling up the ninety-nine steps marked *Réservé Aux Pèlerins Qui Montent À Genoux* ("Reserved For Pilgrims

Who Go On Their Knees"). If the devoted could go upstairs on their knees, I could surely walk up the mountain.

I hadn't planned for my trip to be so very Catholic—being taught that other religions and their churches were part of Satan's Christendom had made me uneasy—but pursuing religion in general was predictable for a former Jehovah's Witness like me. I was curious about people's attachment to idols, even though we were taught to believe that giving veneration to any religious image was wrong. (Once, I found a tiny Jesus, Mary, and cross hidden within a secret compartment in a used wallet I bought at a thrift store and tossed the whole thing in the trash just in case it was possessed.)

While in Montréal, I also visited St. Patrick's Basilica, the Musée des Soeurs de Miséricorde, and the Musée Historique Canadien Ltée (now a Pharmaprix but with statues of the New Testament's Four Evangelists—Matthew, Mark, Luke, and John—still guarding outside). The Musée Historique Canadien Ltée had once been a wax museum that had an exhibit of Christians being eaten by lions. As a child, I was utterly terrified of it and begged Ma not to make me pass by the mutilated faithful.

The Musée des Soeurs de Miséricorde was a convent across the river from where I grew up. As children, my brother, sister, and I were afraid of what happened inside these places but had no idea what that might be. We did know there was a disembodied heart, wax dummies, and mortal women in habits. My great-aunt was a nun, Sister John of the Cross, and had penned some lovely letters to me, even though then I was of a different faith. What could any of these people or objects really do to me?

I did know to be scared of my parents' anger, the way it ripped into our lives with little warning: the violence, the yelling, the leaving. I loved God, but His wrath, images of fire and earth swallowing up the wicked, and the upcoming war of Armageddon were burned into my child's brain. If these prophecies came true, I wouldn't be sailing into paradise on Ma's coattails. Being a child wasn't an excuse—I had to carry my own faithful load.

Was my devotion and faith to Jehovah built on love or fear? Was there a difference?

...

They say that baby ducklings imprint on the first things they see. In my baby pictures, my face is serious, unsure, smiling cautiously, facing the person holding the camera. Most likely my father, but it was Ma I was attached to.

Ma often punished me for getting in trouble at school. It started in kindergarten and continued to grade 1. I couldn't lie to her. She was trying to turn me into a God-abiding, dress-wearing, perfect little girl. A follower of Jesus Christ.

Getting Ma's approval was love to me.

I was two when Ma asked for us to be removed from the Catholic baptismal registry because she no longer wanted to be considered a member of their Church. I do not remember anything that had to do with St. Patrick's Basilica, where I was baptized. I didn't even know the Lord's Prayer, what a Hail Mary prayer was, or how to make the sign of the cross. Ma didn't speak much of her past Catholic life, choosing not to look back.

We were very active in our newly chosen faith. Ma made sure I knew that Jehovah was always watching, but she didn't need to tell me. I felt it.

. . .

When I was six, Brother André's heart was stolen from St. Joseph's Oratory in the middle of the night and held for $50,000 ransom. The church wouldn't pay. The heart was later recovered via an anonymous tip. It reminded me of the pickled brain held in Dr. Frankenstein's lab in the haunted house at Parc Belmont, the one that gurgled, "Help me!"

Before I went to see Brother André's heart, I took a walk in the Gardens of the Way. I came across the sculpture of Jesus at the third station, where he fell for the first time, and it unexpectedly affected me.

I wasn't prepared to have feelings about any of these places, and now in the garden, I felt heaviness in my body, in each step it took. If I had been my old praying self, this would have been the time. But which God would I pray to, the one at my first baptism or the God of my second?

. . .

I saved the Major Reliquary of the Basilica for last. When I got there, it was still daylight, quiet, and there were very few visitors. The gates, thick glass, and an iron grille (with a few handwritten prayers tucked into it) all separated me from the saint's heart in a reliquary jar atop a marble pedestal. When I looked at the urn, its contents were cloudy, and my reflection stared back at me.

I saw the many scenes showcasing Brother André's life. His white iron-framed deathbed with its pencil-thin mattress. All the crutches that had been left behind by the cured faithful. His tomb and original humble beginnings. But his heart wasn't visible to me. I was too afraid to ask the faithful pilgrims nearby if they could see it. After coming all this way, I didn't want to be the one who couldn't.

. . .

"When one has not had a good father, one must create one."
—Friedrich Nietzsche

. . .

When Ma finally kicked out my father, I was fifteen. She'd had enough of his affairs, and he'd had enough of her drinking and breakdowns. We kids welcomed the quiet it brought.

We heard that my father had fought to see us, but little kids' sources are suspect.

After he left, he would take us to Burger King, just like in those typical after-school TV shows. We went to his apartment once, a small place he shared with his friend Johnny. His clothes were lying around the place. He gave us a phone number scribbled on a piece of paper so we could reach him. Later we would only have the phone number of the restaurants he worked at. He would drop by to see us sometimes, but he didn't take us to his place ever again.

"Don't call me Daddy," he warned us when we were out in public.

We wondered if he was part of a gang, or if he had another, upgraded family.

Our inability to separate fiction from reality protected us from the truth we weren't ready to see.

. . .

When I was eleven, I took a short hiatus from the Jehovah's Witnesses after being brought up in "the truth" since I was two years old. To bring me back to the fold, Ma thought it would be a good idea for Tommy and me to study the Bible with a young family from our local Kingdom Hall.

At first, our studies were a joke. We wouldn't pay attention or we'd miss our study times. Then, during one of our Tuesday meetings, I finally made some important connections. I began to understand the prophecies and how they applied to the last days. It was a time of clarity for me, a first in a series of events that would culminate in my baptism and commitment to Jehovah God. I felt warmth and a calm within, whereas before I had been unfocused and without purpose. My beliefs and relationship with Him were now steadfast, and I wanted to serve Him forever.

You can never go back to that one moment when you thought you knew everything.

Once my parents split up, my father didn't seem as interested in us, or me. It was easy to replace my earthly father with a different kind of Father, one who promised to always be there for me. He was the alpha and omega, a God without beginning or end, and He felt real enough to me in prayer that it didn't matter if I didn't know what He looked like or where He came from. After all, the Bible told me in Exodus 33:20, "For no man can see me and live." *The Watchtower* told me God was too powerful to be viewed by human eyes. That we don't see gravity or electricity and yet they exist.

I was young and lost. This language gave me a sense of belonging, meaning, and community. My relationship with God was the main constant in my life that kept me whole. I had finally found a father who would never die or leave me.

. . .

My father doesn't talk about himself or his family much. I often ask too many questions, push the limits of his patience. Should I stop, I wonder? It's taken me so long to get the courage to ask him anything. Like my father, the mirror doesn't tell me who I am or where I come from, but religion had taught me not to question. The answer would be revealed in God's due time. Faith would always have to be enough.

I don't know the exact moment I started wavering from my religion as an adult. I had been an obedient member of the congregation and its doctrine, rarely questioning its truth. I see now that I needed the Jehovah's Witnesses, that I had nowhere else to go, that I needed to feel safe.

I had planned to return. I had the hope that therapy would send me back, fixed and improved. Instead, I ended up questioning my beliefs and whether Jehovah even existed. Anger at God, deep within me, quickly turned to doubt and disbelief. I wonder now if Ma's sudden death all those years ago was a catalyst that would eventually lead to my leaving.

All I know is faith made me see, and then one day it didn't.

GRIEF IS A TOMATO PLANT

"I accept there may never be a day when all
the pieces will be drawn together, and I will see the whole."
—*The Measure of a Man,* JJ Lee

Dirt

I heard somewhere that there are over two hundred bodies on Everest, so, of course, I had to google the number to be sure. I was a skeptic wondering that if this were true why weren't more people talking about it? You'd think I wouldn't have trouble accepting things considering how I grew up. Those belief systems I've chosen to drop, but the spectre of them hangs about like a spider on the windowsill, the one that gets swept away and keeps returning.

I watched a documentary called *Lost on Everest* where Eric Simonson, an American mountain guide, leads a 1999 expedition attempting to find George Mallory and Andrew Irvine, two missing climbers. The pair disappeared trying to climb up to the summit in 1924 and were last seen alive by Noel Odell, also a member of Simonson's expedition.

The *Lost in Everest* crew eventually finds Mallory's body where it still remains today. They placed it under rocks as a sort of burial, away from the elements and animals. They took a DNA sample of his femur and some of his personal effects, and sold pictures of his partially clothed mummified body to the press.

They were unable to locate Irvine.

In the documentary it is explained that attempts to retrieve bodies do happen, but it's often too dangerous and expensive to remove them. I don't know if I am imagining it now, but I thought I heard someone say, "Everest has them now."

Seed

The summer my father became ill, I tried growing tomatoes on my apartment balcony. It was 2021, the second summer of the COVID-19 pandemic, and my regular part-time gig hadn't called me back for work. My dad and I had been talking more and more that year, and the anger I felt when he left us had long cooled. I was no longer a fifteen-year-old kid with abandonment issues.

That summer, I planted tomatoes because I wanted to try my hand at growing something from seed. I planted copious amounts, thinking most, if not all, would survive. Numbers would be the game I'd play.

The first time I tried growing my tomato seedlings, all died, either from a lack of or too much watering. I didn't know that they wouldn't grow back again. I wanted to be surprised so didn't do too much research. I had always avoided plants, besides an odd cactus or two that managed to dry out in my care.

Growing up in the seventies and into the eighties we lived in the Bellerive apartment complex in Chomedey, Laval. We moved from one floor of the apartment building to another, into a small space at first and then into a bigger one. We never had much, but my dad was proud, as if living there among professionals was a status symbol.

My father could be as much fiction as he was non-fiction, so I had the freedom to make up who he was based on what I knew or didn't know. He never asked to read my work, and I didn't share news about what I was writing. I did ask him many detailed questions during our short conversations, about his village name or our family clan, his origins.

My father didn't discuss much of his past life before Toronto and Montréal, even with my relentless queries. I didn't know if he was a city guy or a farm person. I didn't even know where he lived after my parents divorced. Ma didn't say much about it when she was alive.

Later in life, my father gave me tidbits, small stories about him and Ma, how they picked tobacco leaves in Guelph to make some extra money on the way to Montréal, how Ma once slid out of the front seat of the car into traffic because seatbelts weren't mandatory. It was these moments, a few stories that slipped out as he got older, that made me wish that my anger had not made me waste so many years staying away from Montréal. I could not get them back now.

...

It took me decades to find where Ma's ashes were buried, but to be fair I hadn't really looked. In my faith, we cared about a life lived as faithful Christians and not so much what happened to the vessel of our body once our spirit returned to God's memory (or His forgetting, depending on how we had served Him). My sister eventually told me that my father said that Ma didn't want to be cremated, an act that can't be reversed now.

I did attend Ma's viewing and memorial service, but by that time we were mostly estranged. She did try to call us occasionally, even though it was frowned upon. I was following the rules by avoiding her.

For as long as I can remember, it was my heart's biggest wish to be in a television family. I've finally realized that TV families are constructed for entertainment purposes and not based on any type of reality. If I sound jaded, it's because I'm tired of the parts of this story that keep making me tell it to anyone that will listen.

I explain that my mother died by drowning, and I explain again that it was far away from us kids, in Cancun, Mexico, at some resort that doesn't exist anymore. The building that was the resort is no doubt haunted with drownings that didn't begin or end with Ma, the name changed for business reasons, to erase the memory of bad news, death not exactly being a great selling point for the travel brochures.

My brother tells me Ma died on her terms, fighting to stay alive, a story that is still hard for me to hear even after all this time. I was afraid of death as a little kid, thinking I'd be persecuted in God's name and eaten by lions for being a Jehovah's Witness. I was, however, comforted by the fact that death was not final, that I would be rewarded for being faithful.

Ma would not be rewarded. I suppose it was easier to accept this and try to move on. I had to remember that the moment she no longer drew breath she was no longer Ma. I also knew from the Bible's teaching that "the living know that they will die, but the dead know nothing at all, nor do they have any more reward, because all memory of them is forgotten" (Eccl. 9:5). Now that I am no longer a Jehovah's Witness, the scriptures take their time to come to me.

I don't know where my father's ashes went after his funeral. I was afraid to ask my dad's new family about what happened to them.

...

I decided I needed to find Ma even if she couldn't see or hear me. There are some things you just feel called to do. After some research and emails to the Urgel Bourgie funeral home, I was told I could find her ashes an eight-hour drive away, at the Cimetière Laval at 5505, Rang du Bas-Saint-François in Laval, near the place where I grew up.

When I was able to get to Ma's plot, I had no flowers. It was a hot day, and I honestly didn't even know what to say, which is not like me at all. The graveyard was near a farmer's field (actually several fields), and I wondered if it looked like the farm her father had once had, far away in New Waterford—a place she left and rarely returned to, a place she told cautionary tales about.

I couldn't mourn Ma back when she died, partly because of the shock, but also because I was only twenty and full of religion. Now I feel like she often hovers nearby as the writer that she was and wanted to be, the person who I couldn't relate to back then.

She haunts us more in death than when she was alive.

Plant

We were not close, but there was a time I worshipped my father. He was living in Montréal after leaving us, but I didn't know that then. He had a new family and would feed stray cats. I'd be lying if I said I didn't feel jealous of that. He never wanted pets when we were living with him. He always thought them dirty and too much work.

I remember our visits to Montréal's Chinatown as a little girl, when I would hang on to his forefinger and think, *That's my dad, he knows everything, he will always protect me with his black belt, and would never back down from anything.* He never looked behind at what he had lost when he came to Canada.

Like a fool, I believed he'd come to Toronto to visit me like he promised over and over again, summer after summer. Eventually, I accepted that he couldn't come for reasons I'd have to respect.

. . .

My brother, Tommy, sent me a picture of Dad lying in his hospital bed, a thin white blanket covering his body. His eyes were tiny slits fighting to stay open.

Did he wonder if this was real or a dream?

Water

My tomato seeds started off so well, so full of life. A friend told me they're one of the most demanding plants to grow. There is no fixing what I have done or have not done to them.

I read somewhere that when you try to grow tomatoes from seed, they often don't survive. I tried to track where I had made my error and think it was when I left them out in the sun an hour too long while trying to acclimatize them from inside to outside. They were so wilted and droopy, had lost all their form. There was no going back.

Sometimes, I think about how my mother grew up near the water, only to eventually die there too.

Bury

When I was writing my dad's obituary, it felt important that he be remembered by his real name. This would be something I could never write about if he were alive, so I understand why he had to hide who he was. In his things, there were many names, names I hadn't heard of or known.

My father, who already had so many secrets, had yet another and another. He had a whole other family we would find out about—a house, a wife, kids named Dom, Mark and Tanya, a life. He had been a "paper son," meaning false documents had been purchased stating he was related to someone who was already a Canadian citizen or resident. He had even owned a Chinese restaurant in Longueuil.

Everything was out in the open when he got ill and went into the hospital.

When it was decided my dad was going to have heart surgery I pressed for information about his other family. I was worried that if anything happened, I wouldn't know who to go to. For the first time in my life, my father gave me the details, even putting my newly discovered brother on the phone with me. We didn't know each other at all, so it was as awkward as one could imagine. I was both happy and jealous.

When I finally met my dad's other family, we were suspicious of each other but eventually opened up. They told stories of who my dad was to them, and my siblings and I told our stories.

My father was confused as we visited in pairs from each of our respective families. We had to wear masks, but I tried to pull mine down occasionally to show him it was me.

...

The day my father died was like watching a movie.

I had missed an important call about his care because I had been asleep. There had been meetings—more medicine, treatment, and putting out one fire at a time. I think my phone had a ton of missed calls—I can't remember. When I called back, disembodied voices told me it was time, that there was nothing more that could be done.

Unresponsive, unconscious. Someone saying, "I don't want him to suffer." Someone saying, "We will discuss it."

Basically, my dad was dying of everything. His organs were shutting down, he had heart issues, he was bleeding, they were triaging one thing only to have to begin on another.

"Give me time to come down," I said, while tears streamed down my face.

I don't think anyone is prepared to decide something horrible like this. I agreed but didn't know what I was agreeing to.

As Angie, Tommy, and I walked down the hallway, I prepared myself, telling myself I'd be fine; it was almost as if I was disassociating my body from my emotions. I was happy to finally see him without so many tubes and wires, but he was nothing of the man he had been. My brother and sister cried, but I couldn't. I felt my dad's hand and it felt warm, even though that was impossible—the hospital staff had kept him in the morgue as we rushed to get there.

The reality of my father no longer there to listen or blink or squeeze my fingers—I couldn't bear to acknowledge that silence. All I could hear was the closing of hospital doors. I could see nurses with bowed heads looking away. I could feel that I was all alone, just falling into the nothingness. The hallway seemed to go on forever.

We had missed him passing. In fact, he died just as I left the parking lot of my apartment complex. I had taken so long to get my shit together. What did it matter what I wore or how many socks I packed? And now that we were all at the hospital, who was *I* to ask where he would be buried, about his funeral—who was *I* to ask anything?

My dad's second wife took care of all the funeral costs. I admit I was numb and broke, and didn't have much to offer. They discussed the details as he lay there in his hospital bed, dead only a few hours. I wished we could have been more involved in the arrangements, but my husband told me that my family was the second family, the other family. I had to understand that my father had made it that way.

. . .

When I visited my father in the hospital, he would lie there, his eyes open and watering. We would talk about traffic, my writing, his boredom, his cold hands and feet, his sister Helen. He would always shake his head no, that he wasn't in pain. At some point, he could no longer talk because of the trach, the tubes attached to him.

I don't regret going, but I wish I hadn't been naive about the fact that he was dying. I kept thinking he'd get better. I kept saying, like a deluded fool, "We'll be back in a few weeks!"

. . .

I recently watched a documentary about Spencer Matthews, a British television personality who wanted to find the body of his missing brother, Michael. In 1999, Michael had died after reaching Everest's summit, his body never found.

My emotions were already unsteady as I watched Matthews tell the camera that the ten-year-old in him wanted him to find his older brother. As he was interviewed and I viewed footage and pictures, I said out loud, "Please find him." Every time they came across one of the bodies, it was false hope. I could see it in Spencer Matthews's eyes, the original flame dying with each radio call coming up empty. I thought they wouldn't make a documentary without finding him, would they?

When it seemed that finding Michael was not going to happen, the documentary took a turn I didn't expect. The search ended, and instead the team recovered Wong Dorchi Sherpa, a guide that died near Camp Four in 2021. As the family mourned and gave him a proper funeral, it seemed sad that Matthews would not get the closure he needed.

I wonder if Matthews and I are forever trying to get back something that was never ours to begin with.

IN BETWEEN

When I was little, my sister tried to convince me that I came into our family because a Chinese lady had left me in a basket at the door. I felt like I didn't look like my siblings, so she thought it would be funny to tell me this. Part of me believed her story, so I wonder if fear had become a belief.

When you're mixed-race someone's always telling you who you're not. People ask if I'm Chinese, what I am, where I'm "from." If I tell them I'm from Montréal, they say, "No, before that." (I want to say my mom's uterus. Or her vagina. But I can't say impolite things.)

What they're really asking when they ask me where I'm from is who are my parents—*what* are my parents—and it feels like a singling out, an othering. It feels like I don't belong. I am wondering why people think this kind of questioning is okay, why they wonder why I won't engage, won't answer them. This singling out started for me as a child, this "what are you, exactly?"

Once, someone in a train station tried to take me away from my white mother because they thought she wasn't my mother. That's a problem, no? It's happened with me and my white stepdaughter too. People sometimes think I am Indigenous, and will ask if I have a status card, or whatever. It's not friends or people I know well, it's strangers. I don't want to answer because I just don't.

. . .

I took an AncestryDNA test in 2017, just before turning fifty. I wanted to be able to see who I was, what I was made out of, get answers about my background.

The directions were firm: do not drink, smoke, or chew gum half an hour before the test. At $129 a pop, you want to follow the directions. These things make me nervous, so, to be safe, I got Ed to help me. You have to ensure you've got lots of saliva for filling up the provided tube. No bubbles either. I put the sample in the bag and the bag in the box and mailed it off.

I don't know if I took the test because I wondered if Ma and Dad were my real parents. Maybe I just wanted to know for sure. When I got the results back, I didn't even want to read them because there was just too much weight hanging on the answers. I got my husband to read them first: 32% Scotland, 18% Ireland, and the rest of me was Asian—39% Southern China, 8% Central & Eastern China, and 3% Dai.

(Wouldn't that be a great ad for AncestryDNA? A mixed-race woman of Chinese and European ancestry confirms exactly what she was told.)

Most of my relatives on AncestryDNA are white, but I have found very little information on my father's side. I found someone who was adopted, and I told her what I knew, which wasn't a lot. On my mother's side, because she was from Nova Scotia, there were family members from the Scottish Highlands, which I had expected.

So, what did that mean to me when I saw the results?

A friend once said that just because I discovered something about my background doesn't mean I have to do anything about it. I could just have that knowledge. I think that they're right.

. . .

Ayelet Tsabari, my non-fiction writing teacher for a few years, said something to me about writers having questions and needing to know the answers. When I started classes with her, my forays into fiction were long gone, and I hung onto her guidance as I asked my own non-fiction questions and found out there were no easy answers.

I look back at my life in Québec, where language can be an issue, and I realize that I am in-between—in-between religions, in-between my parents, in-between their stories, their telling and untelling, their secrets.

I wonder who claims me, and who I will claim? I don't have a tidy ending, but I didn't really expect one, did I? I am still trying to see what this all means through my writing, making a record as much for myself as I am for someone else.

I guess I'll just figure it out as I go.

TELL ME A GHOST STORY

When I was five, I had a wooden Fisher-Price radio music box that I loved. When I twisted the knob, it would play "Raindrops Keep Fallin' on My Head" over and over. Inside the radio screen were pictures of a little boy and his sister who loved the rain, along with a jumping frog. The music box had a yellow and red plastic carrying strap and the lyrics to the song on the back.

I buried the music box at our local park, in the sand behind the swing set. It was fun to scoop up all the smooth sand with my two hands, covering the radio's yellow face until I couldn't see it anymore.

. . .

My stepdaughter, Avery, is thirteen years old and has been watching *Bones*, a TV show about a forensic anthropologist. Some of the scenes I can't bear to watch with her. Maybe it's the blood, even if it's fake, or maybe it's the sounds of the tools and gloved hands digging or poking around while they're examining the outsides and innards of murdered bodies.

I once fainted after cutting the meaty part of my hand on the ceramic tank of a toilet. I was working a part-time job as a banquet server, and the party was getting rowdy, and the toilet was clogged. I picked up the toilet tank lid, and it slipped out of my hand and broke. I felt along the bottom of the lid, and it sliced me. Water was pouring out everywhere. I panicked and ran to the kitchen downstairs, where the owner saw me holding my hand.

The cut didn't bother me at first, but when I poked the spot where the clean white slice in my skin was, blood started pouring out. I crouched, trying to remain upright, and then went back to the bathroom to put water on my face.

The next moment, I was lying on the cold tiled floor.

In the *Bones* episode "The Donor in the Drink," a man's partially chomped-on body is found in a trout-farm pool. *They are carnivores*, a character points out. Avery loves and is attracted to these shows. She does not turn away like I do.

The shows I watched when I was Avery's age were *SCTV*, *The Littlest Hobo*, *The Beachcombers*, *The King of Kensington*, *Hockey Night in Canada*, and *Magnum, P.I.*—nothing gross. I was into the *Anne of Green of Green Gables* series and *The Thorn Birds*.

Now I love period dramas like *Bridgerton*, *Downton Abbey*, *Pride and Prejudice*, and *Sanditon*, the ones where families love and hate each other, and there are always many secrets. There are forbidden loves, unrequited loves, unwanted suitors, and often a happy ending. Avery will sometimes watch these shows with me—she never says what she thinks about them but doesn't leave when they're on.

Avery can watch disemboweled bodies, but has a hard time with horror and ghost stories. For me there is something about being scared that way that I like. I was never allowed to watch these shows as a kid, so it's a world I am unfamiliar with. Ma even got mad at me for watching the old version of *Star Trek*, which wasn't even that bad.

Unlike many of my peers, I never believed in Santa Claus, the tooth fairy, or the Easter Bunny. Forget the bogeyman. Satan and Jehovah—now they were something to be afraid of.

. . .

I recently binge-watched Mike Flanagan's loose television adaptation of Shirley Jackson's novel *The Haunting of Hill House*. In Flanagan's version, the mother was haunted, the mother was haunting, the mother, the mother, oh, the mother.

It's always about the mother.

I would have followed Ma anywhere knowing what I know now, even if she was just a spectre.

. . .

I have no idea what Avery is hoping to find in her television examinations. I haven't asked her. My religious education told me that after we die, we are "sleeping in death" (1 Thess. 4:13), which was my view, that it was the end until Armageddon and Jehovah resurrect the faithful in the forthcoming paradise. I did not believe in ghosts at all. I was, however, afraid of wicked spirits—former angels who could not return to heaven after the wrath of God's flood, on earth to be with the daughters of men. They had joined Satan and were dangerous, now pretending to be dead, leading people away from God.

When I was young I won tickets from a radio station to see the 1989 film adaptation of Stephen King's *Pet Sematary*. Of course, I wasn't allowed to go because it was considered supernatural. Based on the scriptures, and if I was to stay in God's favour, I had been instructed to follow what Deuteronomy 18:10–11 says: "There should not be found in you... anyone who employs divination, anyone practicing magic, anyone who looks for omens, a sorcerer, anyone binding others with a spell, anyone who consults a spirit medium or a fortune-teller, or anyone who inquires of the dead."

I gave the tickets to my father. I didn't tell him what the movie was about and afterwards he told me he was so scared. I had never known my father to be afraid of anything.

My father used to take us to the Cinéma Electra in downtown Montréal, which played Chinese double features with English subtitles. One movie had the dead hopping to the cemetery to be buried. Known as jiangshi 殭屍 (or hopping corpse), they would haunt and get revenge on the living, and they terrified me. I remember there was a female jiangshi who had a paper talisman over her face and attacked those who had wronged her. The scroll never moved, so you couldn't see what she looked like.

The Cinéma Electra is long gone now. When I first tried to find out what happened to it, there was little evidence it had ever existed. It's taken me years to find out what became of the cinema—I even checked out eBay to see if any memorabilia were left. I asked friends back home in Montréal and looked online in discussion forums but found nothing. Turns out, it shut down in 1978, and the building was demolished in the early nineties, around the time I left.

There's just an empty lot there now. It's like it never existed.

...

I was fifteen when my parents filed for divorce. Ten days before, Québec F1 driver Gilles Villeneuve died in a horrific crash in a qualifier for the Belgian Grand Prix, and it was all over the news. *Le Journal de Montréal*'s headline was "Gilles se Tue à 170 MPH."

The CBC repeatedly showed the accident in the slowest motion. It was not censored, and I couldn't stop watching it. Villeneuve was in his red Ferrari, then airborne, then lying near the fence.

I wasn't surprised at my parents' divorce. With the marriage finally ending, I hoped that peace would fill my father's absence.

. . .

Avery's Xbox used to inexplicably turn on between 12 a.m. and 2 a.m.

We tried to think of an explanation as to why a video game would turn on in the middle of the night—anything that made logical sense.

Avery thinks it was a ghost.

When Avery got a new Xbox console for Christmas, she gave us her old one, and we put it in our bedroom. The console rarely comes on now.

I don't know what to think of that.

. . .

When our mothers died, Avery and I were both asked if we wanted to see them one last time. We both refused. Maybe this is why our mothers are alive in our dreams.

Last night I had a dream that my father was grieving his own father. My aunt and cousins were also there, in a grand house with a long wooden staircase leading to many floors above. When I told Avery about my dream, she wondered if in it my father was dead or alive, and I told her he was indeed alive. She said that this meant he was saying hello. I asked if she ever dreamed of her mother. She said yes, but not often—only twice. My own dreams of Ma are not frequent.

I had a paranormal experience when I went to the Lakeshore Campus of the Humber School for Writers, formerly the Lakeshore Psychiatric Hospital. After decades of putting aside my hopes of being a writer, it was my first time taking writing classes.

One day, the week of my birthday, I heard whispers in the classroom. I looked around and saw no one. It happened one more time, then silence.

I asked later if anyone else had heard anything odd, and they hadn't. Even though I knew there were whispers, I couldn't make out any distinct words. I'd be lying if I said I hadn't immediately thought of Ma, it being so close to my birthday.

Sometimes, I hear Ma's favourite songs on the radio. Bonnie Tyler's "Total Eclipse of the Heart," Foreigner's "I Want to Know What Love Is," Dorothy Moore's "Misty Blue," Bee Gees' "How Can You Mend a Broken Heart?" I don't change the station when it happens. In the days of Ma's drinking, I couldn't listen to the soundtrack of her drunken stupors, but any songs before her addiction took hold or after her recovery, I can bear.

My brother and sister and I have seen many versions of Ma, but we still have not encountered Ma in any spirit form. I wonder if she would come back for revenge, like the female jiangshi. I had, after all, betrayed her in the end.

...

I still talk about Lori with Avery. I'll bring up some random memory, something she said or did. I try to convey that Lori had a tough time growing up.

Lori would sometimes tell me childhood stories, like when she and her sister had to clean all the dishes in the kitchen cabinets, and, when inspected, if it didn't meet their father's expectations, he told them to do it again. Lori and I had similar stories—probably more than I realized. I think about her a lot, perhaps more than when she was alive.

When Avery asks for a Ouija board for Christmas, a Bible warning comes back to me: "Do not turn to the spirit mediums… so as to become unclean by them" (Lev. 19:31). Part of me is afraid because it never ends well when trying to contact the dead.

Ed warns us that if we get a Ouija board, not to do it alone. He has had experience with the dead because he used to live in a haunted house and would hide under the covers in his room as a result. The history of the place was that a pastor and his family had lived there and his little girl had died. There were creaky stairs, lights and TVs turning on and off, and a ghost—a lady wearing a hat passing through their kitchen. When the place was renovated, they found an old picture of her.

We never did buy Avery a Ouija board, and she never said anything about it.

Avery and I still want something from our mothers, something they could not give us in life. If we conjure them up, what will our grief look like once it truly manifests?

…

F1 driver Gilles Villeneuve had a televised, public funeral in Berthierville, Québec, where thousands paid their respects. His coffin was draped in a checkered flag, a signal to drivers that the race was over.

Villeneuve's son, Jacques, was eleven at the time, and there was a moment during the ceremony when he glanced up at his mum, her face unmasked, and he did a double take, suddenly concerned.

What was it like to have everyone watching, to have the burden of sharing their grief with the world? Later, Jacques would say that he hadn't seen his father for two years, that his father hadn't really been a father at all.

...

When I finally dug out my little Fisher-Price radio from the sand, I tried the knob, but it would hardly turn. I could hear it scratching against something and labouring. It no longer resembled anything that sounded like music. I shook it, trying to get all the sand out.

From the outside, it appeared to be fine, but inside the sand had destroyed it.

LEAVE-TAKING

I think we could have been friends if we were not family. I wouldn't have judged you in that way only your children can. Maybe we would have met at a retreat or one of those writing courses you took at Concordia. If I was a drunk, too, we might have met at Alcoholics Anonymous, chatting over stale coffee and cigarettes, newfound addictions to replace the old one.

When you started the meetings, you collected sponsors like some kind of spoon set. I didn't understand the appeal or how it helped. You had friends calling at all times of the day. You liked to drag us to the meetings only to reopen our wounds repeatedly. If you said Richard Bach's line "If you love something, set it free. If it comes back to you, it is yours" one more time, I swore I would throw up on the damn church basement floor. In all those meetings, did you forget to tell them about when you left me, your nine-year-old daughter, at the Eaton's store in downtown Montréal for hours while you drank?

Therapists call this a mother wound, but it feels more like a stabbing.

The truth is, Ma, we were barely friends. The Jehovah's Witnesses shunned you, turning daughter against mother (because apparently that's what Jesus wants).

. . .

These days, people call my former religion a cult.

"Back when I knocked on doors hawking *The Watchtower* magazine, I would bristle if anyone told me I was in a 'cult,'" writes former Jehovah's Witness Daniel Allen Cox. "I'd avoided using the word for fear of it lacking nuance."[1]

In therapy, it took me forever to get through my list of things that were wrong, first with me and then with our religion. I couldn't even talk about who or what I had left. I scoffed and ignored that word *cult*. *No, they're not,* I would say. *They are decent people. I've got friends and family who are still there.* (I don't have to tell you, Ma. You know what you have lost being on the outside now.)

Cults are supposed to be Jim Jones, Charles Manson, David Koresh, and Warren Jeffs, not Charles Taze Russell, a man supposedly following the line of faithful Christians back to Abel. (See, I even remember how to dispel the unbeliever with just a line.)

But yeah, if I'm gonna be honest here, it's a cult.

. . .

By the time I turned seventeen, my drug of choice was the religion that had cast you out. I had it real bad. Once my doctor learned about your history, she told me to be careful about addiction. I told her I don't drink, and I know all too well about Tommy's troubles with drinking and drugs, which I can't blame him for; he's had it rough.

I know I turned my back on anyone who was not one of us—including you. I devoted my time and youth to God, door-knocking

1 "Life after shunning: what I faced after coming out as a queer Jehovah's witness," *The Guardian*, May 10, 2023.

full-time. My life consisted of meetings three times a week, Bible study, preaching, hanging out with other Witnesses, and using my part-time jobs to support myself. In between, you and I would fight about your smoking, your boyfriends, why I was the only one cleaning the house, and what a terrible mother you were. The cockiness of youth and religion can be a deadly cocktail.

Maybe we would have been friends before you went and got yourself drowned on that beautiful day in Cancun, Mexico.

. . .

It's a sunny afternoon, April 14th, 1987, and I am twenty years old. I'm in my yellow kitchen, with its white linoleum floor and speckled green countertops, about to go to the Kingdom Hall. The phone rings, and it's my father.

"Mommy's dead," he tells me, as if discussing the weather.

"No," I say, as if it is negotiable.

(The same plea comes out of my sister's mouth when I tell her.)

People from my congregation call and offer their condolences, but all they really seem to want to know is how you died.

"She drowned," I say in my father's voice.

My friend Allan tells me that I am not behaving normally. I guess he means I should act like a person who just lost their estranged parent, and I'm not. It's strange how people think it's okay to tell you how, what, and when to feel. They want to see drama. They want me to be "weeping and wailing... to be lying down in sackcloth and ashes" (Esther 4:3), a spectacle to behold. No one wants to see who I am now, numb and frozen in my grief.

My older sister cannot call people to tell them the news, so I do. I feel like I owe her this because she always protected me when you were drunk or had your nervous breakdowns, when we were afraid and embarrassed because you were yelling into the hallways of our apartment building. (It always seemed like my older sister was a younger, sober version of a mother.)

I call your best friend Giselle, still reeling from her husband's death, and listen to more nos. I call your sisters, Marg, Joan, and Diane, one by one, and still come out intact.

I am okay, I will be okay, I tell myself, as if by rote. You would be proud that I seemed so strong on those days when really I was falling apart, little by little, piece by goddamn piece.

. . .

After you drown, my eighteen-year-old kid brother, Tommy, and your boyfriend, Owen, are both stuck in Mexico, unable to get an earlier flight home. (You planned to dump Owen after the trip—he ended up wanting your fucking couch, according to the lawyer's letter he sent in the weeks after you died.) Tommy is drinking heavily. Owen is sobbing, inconsolable.

"She's my best friend," Tommy cries, telling me that when he hugged your lifeless shell in the morgue, you were cold, *so freezing.*

The girl sent to us from the Urgel Bourgie funeral home seems too young and happy and not dressed right. The director, the one who only has half a thumb on his right hand, tells us about the state of your body.

"In Mexico, the methods are crude. Her hands are fragile, so we have wrapped her in linen to keep her from falling apart. We don't recommend an open casket."

I imagine him and his half thumb in his antiseptic white office, rehearsing his speeches in front of the Sears portrait of his family. You would laugh at this because you always liked a good joke.

After the brief service at the funeral home, and because you weren't allowed to have a Kingdom Hall memorial, Uncle Danny, your brother-in-law, talks about your former faith and the resurrection hope of returning in paradise. After it's over, the director tells us that your friends have asked to see you one last time. Someone told me not to do this final farewell because when he saw his father's dead body he could not get his face out of his mind. In the end, we say no to friends but let your family enter the viewing room, the door closing behind them.

I believe you're just a shell, nothing inside, that your spirit went back to God, and if He sees fit, you will be resurrected here on the earth in his paradise (John 5:28, 29). I stay behind and convince my older sister to stay with me. Your sister Marg breaks down in the busy Chemin de la Côte-de-Liesse parking lot while cars drive by.

"It is good you didn't go. She looks bloated from the drowning," your niece Joanne tells me.

I stuff my grief down into a hole, bury it deeper.

. . .

It's 2012, and twenty-five years of Aprils have passed when you come to me in a dream. It is only the second time you have ever come to me this way. You ask questions in quick succession. *Who was at the funeral? How did everyone react? Did we read your favourite quote?* I can hardly respond.

I remember clinging so desperately to the dream that I was disappointed you were gone when I woke up. When I tell my brother about it, he cannot suppress sharing the last moments of his trying to save you. I can barely breathe when I realize this is the first time he has given me all the details.

It is only the second day of your vacation, with no clouds in the sky. Owen stays behind on the beach to mind your worldly possessions. The sea is hypnotically blue, and it calls to Tommy—your baby, your last child—and calls to him hard. He is a daredevil. He's always been one.

Come on, Ma. Come on. You follow him.

Suddenly, you both panic because nothing is beneath your feet, and the beach has almost disappeared from your view. The undertow has pulled you out, where the waves are pushing you below the surface. You are not a strong swimmer despite growing up beside the ocean.

You are tired. Tommy knows it. You know it. He calls to you to keep kicking, dog paddle, float, whatever it takes. You are both becoming weaker. The red flags on the beach are becoming so tiny. He is yelling out. He spits out salt water. He must save you. You are drifting away from him. He is tired, so tired.

You are crying. You know you are going to die. He sees it in your eyes.

He gets to you again. Still, he is pushing you up while he goes under; he keeps pushing you up. The water is in his eyes, his nose, and his mouth. It would be so easy to breathe it in. He can hear you calling to him as if through a screen. Your voice is getting fainter. He is getting fainter. He is going under.

People—strangers—are trying to save you. Maybe you tell them, "Get him. Get my son!" and they do. They almost drown too. Maybe your last real thought is *Thank God, thank God they have him. They have Tommy*. Maybe. Maybe your son runs up to you while the crowd gathers.

You're lying on the beach, but shit, you are face down. Everything is happening so fast. People are helping. Compress, compress, compress. You cough up water, and somehow, you are coming to. Still, the crowd continues to grow. *It is so sad, the poor son. The poor mother*, they may say.

The paramedics will not let Tommy go with you. They say they must take you to the hospital. Maybe they tell him *we have to take her now. We must take her, please, please, sir.*

Your eyes will not open. Tommy will not know yet that your chest is not moving, that you will die alone in the ambulance on the way to the hospital because they could not stabilize you. The report will say it was twenty minutes, and then you were gone. You will be in the morgue, and Tommy will demand to see you because he cannot believe it; he will not believe it. They cannot stop him. You always knew he was the type of child that would not and could not be stopped. When they finally let him in, he will touch, hug, and kiss you, but you're long gone. Everything you are is no more. He will remark on the blueness of your skin—something I will never see.

I was the one who was supposed to die, Tommy tells me.

He may not have died that day, but something out there made sure he has been drifting ever since.

. . .

It's a Saturday in November 2012, and I am alone in the bedroom, nothing stirring in the apartment except me. I have been thinking about becoming a mother, and I am terrified that if I do I will not get the good parts of you, only the terrible ones. I am so afraid that I will give birth to something incomplete, someone like me.

I have tried to forget you and pretend I've always gotten along just fine without you, even when you were alive. I couldn't stay in Québec anymore if I were going to move on, and the eight-hour drive to Ontario seemed to be the answer at the time.

I have been watching *Buffy the Vampire Slayer* on the apartment television for weeks now. Today's episode is "The Body," where Buffy finds her dead mother in their house. Joyce, Buffy's mother, is lying on the couch, eyes wide open. I am standing in front of the television, about two feet away, unable to turn it off. I cannot stop watching. I cannot turn away.

It's been twenty-five years since your funeral, and it's time. I can feel the grief pushing out from its hiding place. Everything is telling me to face you. I want to crawl out of my body and escape someplace because I can't stop it. I hear someone sobbing, and it's me. It's me. I'm the one crying. I cannot stop.

You were a poet. After you died, I found hundreds of thin white tissue-like pages of your poems. They filled boxes upon boxes. I do not even remember how they got from your apartment in Saint-Laurent to my duplex in Chomedey. I threw them all out on the curb after the funeral. I even threw out the blue typewriter you used to write them, the one with the missing *R*.

Daddy says you tried hard to publish your poems, but it didn't happen. I'm sorry. I don't know what I was thinking, throwing them out; obviously, I was not thinking at all.

...

You are lying somewhere in the Cimetière de Laval, in Laval. Memories of your funeral come back to me. The sun was shining and life was carrying on as usual, and today is the same. It has taken me decades to find your final resting place, and I am overwhelmed doing so. My friend Carrie, my former Bible student and someone who I would have never met if not for the religion, lives twenty minutes away and knows the way and the area, so she offers to drive. We went through a lot together.

At first, we wander around the graveyard, looking for a map, but there isn't one. I feel like you may direct me, but you don't. There are statues, trees, well-cut grass, flowers, and flat gravestones, which are simple and plain. I go to the office to ask for help, but the manager also has trouble. I scan all the plates on the ground and finally see the letters of your maiden name, covered by grass. I feel guilty that I have not brought anything to leave you.

Maybe if we had met in a different place, time, and life, without all the baggage of me being your child, you would read me a bit of your poetry:

The years kiss each other
Gently—softly—
With a picture of us
Together

from your poem "Reeds and Reflections," and I would be smitten.

That's good, honestly, I would say. *Keep going.* And maybe you would have.

I write "poet" on a small piece of paper from my notebook and bury it in the dirt.

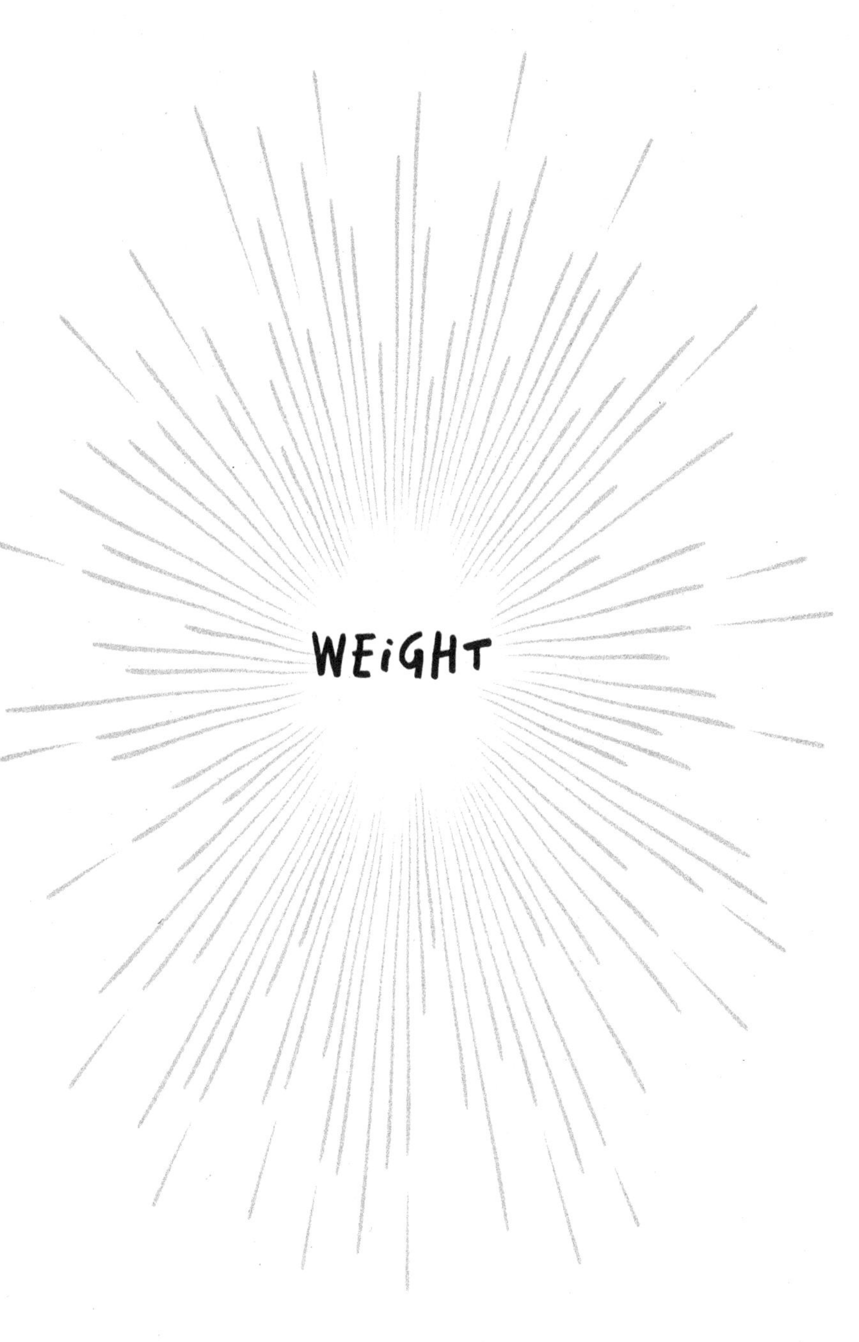
WEiGHT

When I tell Avery I'm making lemon meringue pie,
her eyes get real big.
I pay attention to every single recipe detail,
careful to use brand names and butter, not margarine,
graham cracker crust, just like Ma made.
My mother's pie was always the right amount of tangy lemon,
buttery crust with golden meringue peaks.

Since our mothers both died suddenly, mine by drowning and hers in a car accident, Avery and I both need this memory of what a mother can be.

...

I remember being twenty-nine and baking a lemon meringue pie for a man I had a crush on. I was living with Robin at the time, and the peaks were burnt so bad the tips had to be cut off.

Robin's cookies were never burnt. Her banana bread was moist and cooked all the way through. She's the epitome of the perfect mother.

I wonder if I'm good enough to be anyone's mother.

My husband tells me that recipes are meant to be experimented with and to trust my gut. I grew up Jehovah's Witness so I tend to follow the written word.

. . .

In *The Year of Magical Thinking*, Joan Didion writes, "I know why we try to keep the dead alive; we try to keep them alive to keep them with us."

If I keep Ma a part of my stories, I won't forget what she looks or sounds like, the smell of her purse or the Du Maurier cigarettes she smoked. I won't forget her lemon meringue pie.

The last time I tried to make meringue for a pie, I prepped by watching lots of videos of people separating egg whites. I carefully removed the yolk from shell to shell, making sure the yellow remained while letting the whites slip through my fingers into the aluminum bowl. Not a yellow speck to be found. I took out the hand mixer and placed the beaters in one at a time, then fired it up on medium speed for thirty seconds, just like the box said.

I read the directions over and over and realized I was holding my breath.

I tried to get Ed to do the next steps but he was on the phone. I couldn't wait, so I slowly added the one-quarter cup of sugar, the beater now on high. Two minutes would have to go by to see if it worked. Before the time was up, Ed came over, smiled, and took the hand mixer from my hands to finish. I watched as the meringue quickly became stiff, and then overbeaten.

It had been the best meringue I had ever made and there I was, so willing to give it away.

NOTES AND ACKNOWLEDGEMENTS

Throughout this book I make many references to the Bible. For the most part, I used the 2013 version of the New World Translation of the Holy Scriptures published by The Watchtower Bible and Trace Society. On occasion, because it suited the text, I used the 1987 King James Version.

Versions of the following essays were published in part/whole in the following magazines and journals: "Lessons" in *The Fiddlehead*, No. 290, Winter 2022, BIPOC Solidarities Special Issue, editor Rowan McCandless; "Fiction Baby" in *Tiny Essays*, December 2019, editor D. R. Baker; "Daddy Doesn't Know" in the "Secrets" issue, *Room Magazine*, 41.1, March 2018, and in *Lit Mag Love Anthology 1: Blood & Water*, September 2019, editor Rachel Thompson; "Are You There, God? It's Me, Talking to Mary Karr" in *Body & Soul: Stories for Skeptics and Seekers*, Caitlin Press, March 2019, editor Susan S. Scott; "Saint, Fears. Fathers, Origins: A Diptych" in *The Humber Literary Review*, 2.0, May 2022, editor Leanne Milech; "In Between: Races, Languages &

Religions" in *The Nasiona Podcast*, *The Nasiona Magazine*, January 29, 2021, editor Julián Esteban Torres López.

To all the contests, magazines, volunteers, and judges that read and longlisted or shortlisted my nonfiction and for bringing joy to my inbox: *Room*, gritLIT, *The Malahat Review*, *The Fiddlehead*, Read at the Fringe, Great Canadian Longform's Best of by Rob Csernyik, Edna Staebler Personal Essay Contest Longlist, *The New Quarterly*.

Thank you to Laurie Siblock for her extraordinary copyediting skills. Thank you so much to Marta Balcewicz for her proofreading expertise.

A huge thank you goes out to my publishers, Jay and Hazel Millar at Book*hug Press, for believing in me and my book and taking a chance on me. I appreciate your kind and generous support for my creative endeavours throughout the years we've known each other and for always taking the time to say hello. Thank you for all the hard work you've done in the lit community and continue to do. Other thanks go to Reid Millar, for sales and marketing, and Britt Landry, publishing assistant, for answering all my questions, and everyone on the team behind the scenes.

My dream editor, Stacey May Fowles. I remember being such a fan and getting your newsletter *Baseball Life Advice*, which I read voraciously. Never would I ever have thought I'd get the opportunity to have you as my editor. It meant so much for me to have your guidance, enthusiasm, suggestions, ideas, and gentle prodding to get where I needed to go. I know that *Worldly Girls* would not be in the form it took without you.

Ingrid Paulson for the beautiful typesetting and knock-me-off-my-feet, gorgeous cover.

Family: Ed and S, thank you for supporting my dreams and hopes of pursuing a writer's life. Angie and Tommy. I could not have chosen better siblings and friends and to the other halves, Tanya, Mark, and Dom. Carrie, you're the sister I can never see too much of and don't know what I'd do without. I appreciated the support from my nephews and nieces, Emma, Blake, Victoria, Kaiya & Keana, my sis-in-law Shelley, and aunties Marg, Diane, Joanie, Helen, and cousins Rhonda, Rob, Deb, Joanna, Trish, Tim, Jim, Anita, and Betty. My in-laws Wendy & Ken, who opened their hearts and home to me and always cheered me on. Adam B & Amanda G, Uncle Rowl & Aunt Nancy. My unofficial brother-in-law Rob, and nieces and nephews, Katrina, Bre, and Tristan, for accepting me and letting me be a part of your lives from afar. Sylvia (my Number one fan!), Paul and Janet for making sure I was always included and safe and being fantastic supporters.

Shout-out to my elementary and high school teachers Mrs. Steinberg, Mrs. Sauriol (who let me read my super silly stories), Miss Brown, Abigail Anderson (one of my faves), Fern Butler, and Joan Wasserman. You let this kid who thought she was a nobody feel like somebody.

I am indebted to the Humber School for Writers and my mentor, Erica de Vasconcelos, who gave me one of my first shots of writing confidence after so many years away, and friends Marianne Fedunkiw, William Bonfiglio, Nina Levitt, and Jack Wang, whom I had the happy coincidence of getting to know there and later on because of the program. Our conversations were a gift.

Ayelet Tsabari. I wouldn't be writing non-fiction if it wasn't for you. I learned so much in your class from your lectures, your constructive comments, and your work. Thank you for having faith in me and my words and making me the writer I am today. I'll never forget you.

My non-fiction writing group of special friends: Emily, Leonarda, Lina, Logan, Jagtar, Hege, Laura, and Obim. For your friendship and being there when I was writing and not writing. For always offering an uplifting word for me whether it was in feedback, texts, emails, or calls. I feel like this is your book too.

The Writer's Studio (TWS 2018) and to my mentors Claudia Cornwall, Stella Harvey, and Eileen Cook for helping my stories come along. The seeds of the book really grew in this course. Am so grateful for Ann, Carolyne, Evie, Geoffrey, Maura, and Stewart whose interest and suggestions helped me figure out things. Andrew Chesham and Laura Farina, for being there for me professionally and personally. It was such an honour to be able to learn from and work with you both.

University of Guelph's & University of Toronto's writing courses.

The FOLD (Festival of Literary Diversity), all the staff and volunteers and director Jael Richardson: The FOLD made it possible for me to see myself in books and community. Thank you for all you do.

Nicole Breit: When I was finally able to take your course, it was through a challenging time. I had some stories that had to be coaxed out of me, and I knew it would have to be with your containers. Thank you for your friendship, introducing me to work that would make me create differently, and letting me find my artistic side again.

Chelene Knight: Your enthusiasm, praise, and edits for *Worldy Girls* in its earlier forms was such a blessing and let me know I was on the right path. I appreciate your mentorship while I was with *Room* and in all the ways you continued to offer guidance outside of it.

Pamela Mulloy and Susan L. Scott and *The New Quarterly (TNQ)*: Thank you both for being such champions of my emerging work from the beginning and for making space for me and my spiritual writing in the different forms it took. Susan, I know that the Mary Karr story would not have happened without our many conversations, ideas, and your encouragement.

Rachel Thompson: Thank you, Rachel, for giving me your guidance, friendship, and unofficial mentorship. I learned so much. Grateful for all of it; everything.

Tom Hart: Tom, you took a chance on me and made me surprise myself. I felt such joy at The Sequential Artists (SAW) and learning from you and the program.

Other editors and fantastic mentors: Crystal Chan, Annahid Dashtgard, Alicia Elliott, Jen Ferguson, Kathy Friedman, Eufemia Fantetti, Chelene Knight, Jónína Kirton, Amanda Leduc, JJ Lee, Carrianne Leung, Eternity Martis, Rowan McCandless, rob mclennan, Leanne Milech, Sharon Miki, Dominik Parisien, Sarah Selecky, Sanchari Sur, Phoebe Wang, Lindsay Wong, and Zoe Whittall.

Supporters and more friends along the way and more (I also felt my literary life flashing before me): Melissa Anderson, Anomaly, *Augur Magazine*, José Miguel Contreras Avendaño, Balderdash Reading Series, Manahil Bandukwala, Chris Baranieski, *Carte Blanche*, Megan Beadle, Susan Bentley, Selina Boan, *Bookish Radio*, Anna Bowen, Tina Brobby, Monica Calderon, Conyer Clayton, Megan Cole, Doris Corcese, Julia Cottrelle, Daniel Allen Cox, Molly Cross-Blanchard, Amber Dawn, Kim

Davids Mandar, Charlotte Donlon, Leanne Dunic, EW Reading Series, Andrew Faulkner, Federation of BC Writers Summit, Sierra Skye Gemma, Hollay Ghadery, Sahar Golshan, Leah Golub, Shazia Hafiz Ramji, Frank Hansen, Rachelle Hansen, Jenny Heijun Wills, Charlotte Henay, Jeremy Luke Hill, House of Anansi, Inkwell, Invisible Publishing, Erica H Isomura, Mahak Jain, Zilla Jones, Preeti Kaur Dhaliwal, Nailah King, Larissa Lai, Yi Shun Lai, Margo LaPierre, Amanda Leduc, Catherine (Cat) Lewis, Anna Ling Kaye, Juliette Yu-Ming Lizeray, Annick MacAskill, Melanie Mah, Derek Mascarenhas, Farah Mawani, Alissa McArthur, Coco McCracken, Catia Mendes, Mridula Morgan, Rose Morris, Teresa Moon, Karen Murray, Nav Nagra, Leigh Nash, Shelagh O'Neill, Lue Palmer, Kimmie Panneton, Platform Reading Series, Adam Pottle, Deepa Rajagopalan, Evelyn Rubia, *The Rumpus*, Scout Ruppe, Salma, Seema & Ibi Saadi, Aileen Santos, Lori Sebastianutti, Geffen Semach, Jane Shi, Tartan Turban Reading Series, Maša Torbica, Simpson, Jen Sookfong Lee, Arielle Spence, Laurian Soper, Erin Soros, Tammy Stairs, Steffler, Surrey Muse, Gillian Sze, Kelly S. Thompson, Linda Trinh, Emily Urquhart, Peter Vaillancourt-McIver, University of Toronto Hart House, Shristi Uprety, Laura Vrcek Capilitan, Vocamus Writers Community, Isabella Wang, Yilin Wang, Wild Writers Festival, Allison K. Williams and Binder Full of Memoirists, Jules Wilson, and Kayi Wong.

Banff fam forever: Aleyda, Andrea, Brandon, Cale, Carla, Chanel, Deepa, Dina, Ida, Joyce, Kara, Katherena, Leif, Steph, Tanya, and Xen.

LitMag lovelies: Sophie Afriat, Amanda Bishop, Lyndall Cain, Ellen Chang-Richardson, Heather Diamond, Whitney French, Yolande House, Dawn Hurley Chapman, Julie Hart,

Shirley Harshenin, Eve Krakow, Margaret Nowaczyk, Deanna Partridge-David, Rachel Laverdiere, Kimberley Peterson, Kerrie Penney, Shan Powell, Laura Sergeant, Set Shuter, Meli Walker, Candace Webb, Sharon Dale Wexler, Angela Wright, Lacey Yong, and Karen Zey.

The Doubles baseball fam: Becca & Bobby, Ben & Janine, Dani & Craig, Holly and Heather, Jamie & Lory, Liz & Peter, Ryan & Renee, Tyson & Mel, Jeff & Amy, Nick & Jody, Meera & Rob, Michelle & Brad, Pachenga & Graham, Scott & Brandy and all the littles. My first hockey team; Chiropractic Works, coaches Brad and Neil, Alison V, Jenny M, Louise Jefferson, Red Bull, Sue, and Princess, The Originals II in various forms and players, and the Soccer Roos for teaching me what it's like to be part of a team, to win, to lose together, and have fun.

My lovely time at *Room Magazine* and a shout-out to all the Roomies I met and worked with during 2018–2021, who helped me become a better writer and literary citizen.

Also, thank you to: A&K, Astrina Rassias, Boonie & S, Chinn, Danica Longair, Dave & Di, Debbie Bateman, Doug & Marilyn Davies, Hope Lauterbach, Jessica J, Jill Maynard, John Wenzel, Jojo, Justin Ancheta, Karen McCall, Kaye, Kelcey Parker-Ervick, Kelly-Anne Maddox, Kerissa Dickie, Kim June Johnson, Kim Spencer, Linda Yip, Lori D for long convos, Louise Dowd and kidlets, the Laws, the Menahems, Micheline, Michelle Marie Premura (in memory of), Natasha & Johnny, Rapson, Robin, Sally Keefe-Cohen, Simona Vaserman, Sue Nuttall, Terri Taylor, and Linda Zwicker.

Good times with the M Marketing team of Carolyn, Chuck, David, Julie, and Tara, and the other M team, Anca, Barb, Carrie,

Joni, Lindsay, Maria, Marion, Michelle G (my early fan!), and Sharon.

The GC Elements crew for being so awesome and letting me lead a creative writing life and cheering from the sidelines, Adam, Ashley, Cheryl, Courtney, Donna, Ethan, Heather, Jason, Jenn M, Jess, John, Karam, Krista, Lana, Manoj, Nadine, Noel, Rachel M, Richard, Ryan B, and Stu.

In memory of Lori. Thank you for the blessing of your kid who made me the mum I never thought I could be.

Books and writers that showed me some of the way: *How to Write an Autobiographical Novel,* Alexander Chee; *Paper Shadows,* Wayson Choy; *Lit: A Memoir,* Mary Karr; *An Unquenchable Thirst,* Mary Johnson; *Lies My Mother Never Told Me,* Kaylie Jones; *The Secret Lives of Bees,* Sue Monk Kidd; *Dear Current Occupant,* Chelene Knight; *Watch How We Walk,* Jennifer LoveGrove; *Tell It Slant,* Brenda Miller and Suzanne Paola; *A Stranger's Journey,* David Mura; *Lullabies for Little Criminals,* Heather O'Neill; *A Complicated Kindness,* Miriam Toews; *Educated,* Tara Westover; *Out of the Blue,* Jan Wong.

I am grateful for the support of the Writers' Union of Canada and the Ontario Arts Council.

Thank you to all the libraries.

Thank you for your care, Dr. Meinig, Dr. Ticoll, Dr. Greenaway, Muriel, Laura, and Phương. Y'all gave me what I needed and in so many ways saved my life.

If you or someone you care about is thinking about suicide, please call or text 9-8-8 (within Canada); available 24 hours, 7 days a week, all year.

PHOTO: DEEPA RAJAGOPALAN

TAMARA JONG is a Tiohtià:ke (Montréal) born writer of Chinese and European ancestry. Her work has been published in the *Humber Literary Review*, *Room Magazine*, and *The Fiddlehead*, and has been both long- and shortlisted for various creative non-fiction prizes. She is a graduate of The Writer's Studio at Simon Fraser University, and a former member of *Room Magazine*'s collective. She currently lives and works on Treaty 3 territory, the occupied and ancestral lands of the Haudenosaunee, Anishinabewaki, Attiwonderonk, and Mississaugas of the Credit First Nation (Guelph, Ontario). *Worldly Girls* is her first book.

COLOPHON

Manufactured as the first edition of
Worldly Girls
in the fall of 2025 by Book*hug Press

Edited for the press by Stacey May Fowles
Copy-edited by Laurie Siblock
Proofread by Marta Balcewicz
Type + design by Ingrid Paulson

Printed in Canada

bookhugpress.ca